Allowing Magnificence

Living the Expanded Version of Your Life

Susan Winter

ISBN: 1-4791-7608-7
ISBN-13: 9781479176083

Dedication

This book is dedicated to the courageous and loving soul that lived within the woman I knew as my mother.

TABLE OF CONTENTS

Acknowledgements

It is with gratitude and heartfelt thanks that I offer my deepest appreciation to the following people who have been instrumental in this book's publication: To my beloved friend Alexander de La Tremouille, I thank you for your immense support in continually fueling the vision I seek to create and for keeping me aligned with that goal. You are my North Star. To Steven Vincent, Donna Amato, Laura Banks, Steven Gustave, Barbara Karo, Delio Pacifici and Sonia Brazao: thank you for the supreme gift of your friendship, your faith in my abilities, and for trusting my guidance.

To Oprah Winfrey, the first host and interviewer who truly heard my words and resonated with my thoughts, I thank you. You gave me the opportunity to speak on behalf of those who had no voice; couples who'd been invalidated and reviled for a type of loving partnership that had been greatly misunderstood. And, for illuminating that true love (regardless of its form) is a divine gift that is to be honored and respected. In releasing those couples from societal judgment you created the greater possibility of love, for all. For this gift, I have no words within the human language to express my level of gratitude.

Special thanks go to two extraordinary clients: Sorina Gabriela Marinescu and Cory Parker Cabral. You have both shared your hearts with me. I thank you for allowing me to be of service to you. Great thanks goes to my proofreader Esther Forrester, for the many hours of work and dedication you have provided. And to my amazing tech guru Johnny Ricco, your ongoing support and assistance has been amazing. Your astounding talent has allowed for the expansion of my message as we continue to discover new platforms for its expression.

Preface

I've written the book I wanted, but never found. It addresses the issues many of us have who are conscious and aware, yet experiencing obvious gaps between what we know and actually applying that information to our day-to-day lives.

This book was written for people such as myself: those of us who've done our inner work. We've taken the classes, read the books, and attended the workshops. We know the major Principles of Higher Consciousness. We understand that we create our reality from the thoughts we think and the beliefs we hold. We've amassed numerous tools in our spiritual/psychological/philosophical toolbox. Yet, we can still have those moments when an outer event catapults us into an emotional state of turmoil and confusion. No matter how great our toolbox we begin to question the merit of all this "knowledge" we possess. This book identifies the missing links needed for our safe return to serenity, reconnection to our Truth, and the greater Truth.

I've chosen to present this information in a format I find preferable for easy assimilation. It's potent and compact. Like myself, I doubt you have the time or patience to read on and on for 15-20 pages before getting to the meat of the subject. Tell me what I need to know, get to the point, give me the tools, and give me hope. With concise chapters designed for easy absorption, the information provided details the exact manner to correct the existing condition in thought and action.

Allowing our magnificence to shine forth is a process of uncovering our own perfection. It's the exquisite realization that *we* are our greatest asset and knowing that we have always been connected to our Truth. Without this inner wisdom all the pretty words written within a book are ineffective. The Self is our foundation. It is crucial that we understand how to see ourselves clearly and see the world of outer occurrences for what they really are. When we identify the greater form of ongoing architecture that is here to aid us, we begin to taste a sublime freedom. In learning how to read that architecture we begin to understand "why things happen." Only then may we live the perfection of who we are, and who we came here to become.

Introduction

There is no book written and no course taught that can be effective if we are not connected to the power of our true selves. When we cannot see ourselves clearly, there is no possibility of seeing others (and life's events) with clarity. To allow our magnificence is to liberate the true self and see life through a clean, clear lens.

The purpose of this book is to give you that missing information: the truth about who you are, and why things happen. These are the two subjects that cause the greatest amount of human suffering and confusion. Every person who passes through this life will, at some point in time, find himself or herself asking the following questions:

1. How can I live the life I desire?
2. Why are certain things happening to me?

Answering these questions and providing effective tools to discovering the answers are the missing links that merit inclusion in any discussion on attaining personal happiness and abundant living. Living the life you desire is predicated on knowing how to reconnect to the limitless power you already possess. That is your eternal freedom. It is the gift you give to yourself and the gift you give to the world. You own it. You have it now. Its realization has been hidden by the errant thoughts you've adopted along your journey in life.

To live the life you desire requires unlocking the True Self. Allowing your life to work for you is the natural outcome of realizing that *you* are your greatest asset. The "real you" is already perfect. You don't need to create a new you. You don't need to alter the image of who you think you "should be" to match the standard of the world in which you live. Allowing magnificence is far easier than that. You only have to uncover the authentic Self that lives within, and let that gem shine. It can (and will) do so, when you become aware of every thought that is not in correspondence to what you see in your mind and what you desire in your heart.

When the life you are living is less than what you want, that is a clear indication that your thinking has been limited by external messages. Absorbing thoughts that are not true for you, or not the truth about you, is the aspect of your life that is amiss. You're not faulty, less than others, or off the mark. Your thinking is off the mark. Your beliefs about "who you are," your value, and how you appear to the world and others, is the information that is amiss.

This can be remedied. It's not hard work, but it does require some backtracking to find the original errant messages that were formed in your past. Once those limiting beliefs have been uncovered, you will be living the boundless freedom of your authentic life. You will be united with your True Self and know the unrivaled perfection of living the fullest expression of your life.

To live a life without limits is to live with the understanding that all events and situations are here for our benefit. Translating that awareness into real-life application can be daunting when confronted by an extreme challenge. In the midst of a massive drama, it's easy to doubt the validity of this precept. How can we detect a benefit in the case of betrayal, abuse or cruelty? The physical aspects of the events seem so real and meaningful, that we are captivated by its spell of presentation. When our eyes and minds remain locked upon the observance of the event, the analysis of its characters, and the story of its meaning; then we will never find a benefit (or reason) for its occurrence.

The key to unlocking the gift within all that occurs lies in "looking again" at what we think is the reality of the situation. Are we absolutely certain there's nothing else within this given "story," that we might be missing? Are we extracting the correct information from what *appears to be* happening? Could it be that the situation, no matter how horrific it appears, is here to advance our lives and create an unforeseen future benefit? In asking these questions, we open the door to discovering the gifts that lie hidden beyond the chaos and pain we are experiencing. It is there that we find our answers. Those answers light our way in the darkness and direct our journey toward our true liberation.

There is no secret that's being withheld from us. The world, and all its actions and events are completely transparent. Life is constantly presenting its truth to us. It is everywhere, in every moment and in every occurrence. The reason "why" things happen to us is so obvious, that we fail to see it. Uncovering the gift within all that transpires necessitates our looking through the given situation with a new set of eyes; eyes that see beyond the physical dance of *appearance* and through to the underlying purpose of the event. In reading those messages and instructions, we find we are finally free. When we are free of guilt, blame and self-reproach, we may now live the expanded version of our lives.

When we look at the challenge again, with new eyes, we see there is an amazing and benevolent design that is working on our behalf. Events/situation are only the set-up and vehicle by which the information is presented. We begin to detect the beauty within the apparent chaos and see the gift in all that is occurring. We meet life's challenges with confidence and stability, knowing the exact reasons for each event. We begin to see the blessings in the midst of the chaos. We discover the twists and turns of life have their own wisdom, as we now utilize that information for its intended purpose. We gain the missing links that we lacked and learn how to live the expanded version of our lives.

PART ONE
The Architecture of Liberation

Chapter 1
A Pattern Emerges

There are two categories of people in this world: those who live their lives reacting to life's events, and those who live proactively as a result of the events they experience. The latter group of individuals utilizes every situation they encounter to gain greater awareness and propel their personal advancement forward. Life is seen an opportunity to refine oneself while creating an expanded reality.

This line of thinking is the result of keen observation and insight. In the maturity and mastery of this conscious observation a stunning discovery is made: nothing is random. There is a pattern to all events that occur. What was once an impressionistic image of life now comes into clear focus. There is a definitive framework of assistance that is working for our benefit. As we continue to gain greater clarity, we begin to see that each segment of our life's journey has been perfectly crafted for our evolutionary enhancement.

This ongoing architecture is constantly working to aid us and move us closer to our True Selves and to the greater truth that life is purposeful and benevolent. We hold in our hands the ability to create a marvelous reality when we are able recognize the patterns of assistance and understand that in every moment, we have backup and aid. We aren't a mass of confused and sorry souls floundering in the midst of the violent unknown. We are humans experiencing the exact situations required to advance our self-understanding and greater participation in this world. We are here to learn, grow and contribute within the guidance and protection of a wiser construct.

We can become active participants within this grand convergence. We can trust the ongoing enactment of all outer forces that come to spur our conscious awakening. By acknowledging and incorporating this enhanced form of thought, we are able to open ourselves to the fullest possibilities that lie before us. Freed from the template of our smaller vision, random events and meaningless actions reveal themselves to be of glorious benefit, as vehicles for our enlightenment.

The design of this architecture is flawless. The magnificence of this realization confirms that there is a purposeful intention to the flow of life. Created to activate our highest expression and greatest contribution, we begin to see all of the events in our lives as vehicles for transformation and liberation. We comprehend the gift in all that transpires.

There are no mistakes. Every step we took brought us to where we now stand, which is perfectly choreographed for our next movement. There are no lost, wasted, or irrelevant relationships, careers or beliefs—only the internal honing device that constantly seeks to perpetuate our ultimate evolution.

All things seek to transform us into the greatness for which we were designed; the highest love, the richest life, and the fullest creative expression of our individuality. That is the inherent gift of a divine architecture that seeks our ongoing expansion within the power of an exquisite design, intent on helping us realize our higher self.

It is the unfolding of our true self, the crystallizing of our clearest intent and its active integration into this life that is our gift. This gift is twofold. It is a gift we give to ourselves and a gift we give to the world. It is the stewardship of this consciousness that is born simultaneously with our birth.

Chapter 2
The Gem Within

Everything starts with the Self. The life we live begins with us. The thoughts we think are formed, filtered and interpreted through the self. It is the self: our identity, our attitude and understanding, which flows outward to everything we touch. When the self is healthily integrated and cleared of false limitations we are free to express our highest vision. The origin of all outer action is born from the gem within us.

If we want anything to change in the outer world, we must change. It is our energy that determines what qualities we infuse into the life we've been given. It is our intention that ignites higher outcome. It is our love that liberates others.

We are what we believe to be true about ourselves. We can be bloated with false ego or humbly aware of our contents and open to constant improvement. We can be filled with envy, hate and jealousy, or love, truth and generosity. Whenever we look outside of ourselves we will find the reflection of our inner beliefs. As we clear the layers of false beliefs that confine us, we clear our ability to see through the illusion around us. Without the tools to uncover the gem within, we will only see artifice when looking at the magnificent.

To those individuals who feel they belong to the "group that has no group," seeking a matching reflection in the outer world is useless. There is only the unique image of your own individual majesty mirrored back from the core of your true self. Without the benefit of corresponding reflection in the world, one's self-image may feel faint in form. It is not. It is an addition to all that exists and heralds the dawn of greater expansion, as the world must expand in accordance to its appearance.

The task of uncovering the true self is unique to our mission in life. We were not born to become carbon copies of other people's lives. We were not endowed with creativity, passion and dreams to follow the dictates of a world that would have us lessen our greatness to fit into an existing template. Seeking authenticity is often an unsupported journey. It is in the journey of uncovering the true self that we discover our true purpose in life.

Chapter 3
Learning to Forget

As great souls innately connected to our truth, we entered this world in diminutive form. We knew when we were hungry or tired. We knew what we liked and didn't like. In the process of socialization we acquired the skills to walk, speak, read, write and adapt to our surroundings. In learning the basic skills by which to participate in this great new world, part of us also learned to forget.

We took on identities formed in correspondence to our parents, siblings, and community. While the necessary foundation needed to function within society was being born, there was also a small death of our internal connection to the Self. Our original connection was clear and primal. In this process we began to alter our Self, to accommodate the greater world at large. Inner knowing became clouded by the dictates of others. The first layers of necessary socialization were also the first layers that shrouded the gem within.

Socialization taught us that there were consequences for our actions; that actions not only affect ourselves, but others. We shouldn't touch a hot stove or taunt our little sister. Transforming impulses into manageable behavior tempered our primal emotions with discernment and compassion. To function and participate in this new world we were instructed on how to handle power, anger, submission, desire and cooperation. The first external blueprint was formed. In the process, vital inner directives were muted.

As the small, still voice slowly faded to allow for this new input, an amalgamated identity was formed. This identity had its own power and knowing, but was tainted by other messages as to what we can and should become, and how that future person looks in the outer world.

In looking outside ourselves for the answers we learned to forget our own truth. Yet, at the same time we sensed an inner urging. As the original connection to our truth became fainter in favor of this "other" truth, we felt an equal desire growing within that demanded expansion. The dampening of our internal voice compelled us to seek our truth, once again.

Why would a bounteous system of architecture set up barriers to finding our way back to wholeness? Wouldn't it be more effective to start whole and remain intact? The wisdom lies in the knowledge that the sweetness we're seeking is found in the journey of rediscovery. Only when we have lost ourselves do we appreciate the value of finding ourselves. Only when we have challenged our abilities do we feel worthy of the identity that was innately ours. Upon the discovery of our forgotten gift, we value it and know it is eternal.

We have come here, in physical form, to take on the teachings of a physical reality. The buffet table is full of dark and light, challenges and victories. We were designed to express our greatness in a world complete with struggles and rewards. Never forgetting the remnant knowledge that we are perfect and whole, intuition and inner guidance are our allies. It is in temporarily forgetting, that we are urged to remember what has been encoded within in our heart.

Chapter 4

Our Greater Design

The first step to discovering our true self lies in understanding that we've been indoctrinated to accept "limitation" as a valid construct. Limited thinking is a foundational principle in our given thought structure and its auto-analysis. Erasing this databank of inferior information is the beginning of personal freedom and liberation. We are more than what we've been told. We can be more than what we've been told.

In order to actualize our greater design, we have to readjust our own internal wiring. Without re-examining our internal beliefs, all the daily affirmations and visualizations will fail to render their desired results. No outer change is possible while tethered to underlying misconstructions. We are not faulty, or defective. We've just been seeing life through a distorted lens. That lens limits the elegance of a natural design that is here to elevate us.

Perhaps we've experienced individual moments of great creation. Our desires unfolded effortlessly. Reaching constancy requires internal alignment, and realignment. Remembering those moments where we've caught a glimpse of a spectacular outcome: the recognition of an unbounded opening to a greater force at work transforms hopeful wishes into known beliefs. The capacity to understand an expanded reality is far more tangible in those glorious examples of clarity.

Apart from a single moment of awareness that puts all the pieces together and vanishes, there is a concrete system to replicate these experiences with greater frequency. It begins with "Open Thought" and continues with solidification of the true self. Open Thought is the ability to see *beyond the apparent*. It allows for alternative answers to formerly automatic assumptions. It allows for greater contextual understanding that moves beyond black and white thinking. The true self is the solid compass by which we see clearly and without limitation. Wisdom is innate. There is recognition, deep inside, when we touch what is real. There is no resistance. There is comfort and familiarity in the extraordinary. Those are the hints, the nudges we keep secret in our hearts and put in a box titled "something else that cannot be explained, but exists."

The structure of a greater design places a series of beautiful patterns in motion that correspond to a finer dimension of reality. It isn't just a dream, or a hope. It is a new reality that growing numbers of individuals are experiencing in small and grand ways. It is the knowledge we can't explain, and the gut feeling that guides us with precision. It's the instinct that tells us the person we've met has a purpose in our lives, the opportunity we've encountered isn't accidental, and that in all these mysteries there is a force guiding us. Serendipity and luck transform into purposeful intention. Proof of a divine architecture becomes evident.

Chapter 5
Other-Minded

As a child, I'd always felt different. Reality, as presented by those around me, never matched the story I saw in my own mind. The explanations, interpretations and directives given were in complete opposition to my natural instincts. As an American child (who only spoke English) life was like watching an Italian film with French subtitles. There had to be something wrong with me, as the greater majority of humanity seemed to be in contextual agreement.

In order to function effectively and fit into the world I observed, I began to amend my version of reality. Yet, I wrestled with this incongruity. Hearing my voice pitted against the voices of a world that spoke so loudly and insistently in union, I wondered why I couldn't get in harmony with those around me. I envied their ease at checking off the tasks that ensured success. Right school, check. Right career, check. Right partner, check. Right home and right social group, check and check. What was this urging inside that fought for freedom and yearned for an unscripted life? Why this innate insistence upon seeing life with fresh eyes and an unbiased perspective? I hadn't yet accepted the fact that I was wired differently from others. My compass was aligned with another set of values and desires. It reminded me of the times I'd tried to borrow someone else's reading glasses. While in theory they should work, they weren't my prescription.

In looking at a world that isn't in resonance with our core, the images that should be clear are blurred by the fact that they're seen through a lens that isn't ours. The purpose of this book is to allow those who see and interpret life differently to embrace the vision they hold, and utilize the beauty of a continual design that fosters the progression towards the advancement of this realization.

We've come into this human experience to add our specific compositional qualities to the world. Not to be seen as untenable, but rather as additional possibilities that can extend the existing options. The result is expansion. In that manner, life becomes richer. Rather than a bland set of predictable choices life becomes imbued with exhilarating options.

Chapter 6
Last Card in the Deck

By my twenties I'd expanded my worldview to include metaphysical thought, eastern religions and psychology. I had a better set of guidelines but the underlying incongruity persisted. Though I had a larger set of tools at my disposal, my inner conviction was still illusive.

Then the day came, late in life and long overdue, when I gave up. I gave up trying to be what I'd been told to be and shifted my interpretation of reality. Every method I'd studied worked a little, or only in certain cases. Nothing felt truly consistent. The books I'd read provided inspiration that lasted the length of the read. The tools belonged to others, and came from an ideology that sounded good in theory but failed the tests of day-to-day living. Fed up, frustrated and with nowhere else to look for answers, I did it. I took the leap. I played the last card in the deck: mine.

What if this incredible system of life came with its own manual? And, what if we all had access to the manual encoded within ourselves? I'd listened to the world and clearly they weren't happy. I'd listened to mystics removed from everyday life. I'd listened to new thought, conventional thought and everything in between. I chose to trust myself and let my own guidance tell me what to do. The direction I took was the opposite of everything I'd been told. The answers I got were in opposition to all I'd been told. While that, in and of itself, could have caused a greater lack of confidence, I never felt more sure of anything in my life. For the first time, I felt safe and comfortable with my actions and inner directives. They didn't match any script or doctrine. They were my choices, clear and confidently chosen regardless of how they were seen by anyone else.

When in doubt about what action(s) to take, I would ask myself what to do. Following my own instructions resulted in choices I'd never seen before or thought were possible. Without fail, my internal choice was in direct opposition to all my previously learned instructions. It was the wild card. Stunned by the power of its direction and effect, it was not only a better choice for me but for all parties involved. Novel, unexpected and unanticipated, I'd found the first consistent tool for general application in day-to-day life. It was to erase everything I'd been told.

When the idea of erasing everything we've been told is first presented, it may appear that doing so will leave us bereft of guidance. That is not the case. Human beings have been pre-programmed with a magnificent inner computer, possessing intelligence beyond our finest imagination. This internal system is limitless in its ability to rack up incoming data and assess the best method of approach to any given situation with ease. Processing the entire picture beyond conscious comprehension, this internal computer sees life clearly, and free of distortion. Grounded in alignment, decisions and resulting actions are no longer laborious or difficult tasks. It doesn't take us years to activate our internal computer. It can be up and running in a matter of seconds. It is our conscious knowledge of our inner computer's existence that reboots our internal programs and allows for its download, automatically.

Chapter 7
Erasing the Databank

I ran into my friend, Steven, when leaving my apartment one crisp, cool day in October. His fortieth birthday was approaching soon. He'd decided to ask all his friends for their best advice about what to do upon entering this new chapter of his life. Without hesitation I said, "Erase everything you've been told as quickly as possible. Begin living your real life." His head tilted back as he roared with laughter. "Why? What have you been told by everyone else?" I asked. "Oh... things like get good health insurance and open an IRA."

While Steven received good advice from his other friends, it came from a different perspective and a different program. Steven "got" my answer. He'd had many lives in his brief forty years—from insanely rich and influential to nearly homeless. From activist to social philanthropist and atheist to spiritual mentor, he'd devoured every book known on thought systems and philosophical/spiritual tenets. As a walking library of collective information on belief systems he saw the bigger picture, and laughed in agreement.

We have been living under the false belief that if we erase all we've been told about what is the "correct" way to live our lives; we'll be left with no basis from which to function. The opposite is true. We have come into this life encoded with the truth about whom we are and have been given an inner-compass that knows our true north. We've been blessed with instincts, intuition, and a mind capable of tabulating input to decipher choice and consequence. This same incredible system has provided humans with a body that automatically strives to heal itself. If we witness a cut healing on our body, why would we think the greater directive of life wouldn't also have the wisdom to manage our course of action?

We've also been led to believe we must take in a whole system of thought, in order to achieve the desired success we seek. Who made that rule? Why do we believe it to be true? We have no problem ordering A La Carte from a menu. Why don't we think we can pick and choose from those ideas within various thought systems that resonate for us, as well? If a certain system of philosophical/ psychological or spiritual thought works for us, then we may utilize it. But, we may also choose to erase some or all of it, and live from our own menu.

There are no "shoulds." Whatever works for you, works for you. If and when any system of thought no longer feels effective, try something else. Eliminate what feels counterproductive and/or add new components that resonate for who you are becoming at that time. Allowing choices to be fluid allows for the inclusion of new input. In that way, there is alignment with the greater evolutionary directive of Life.

PART TWO
Accessing the Higher Self

Chapter 8
Inner Tapes

How did we build our current identity and inner beliefs? It began when we were children and continued to develop as we were socialized into forming beliefs about ourselves in contrast or similarity to our greater world. The inner tapes we hear in our heads, otherwise known as our beliefs, were formed in reference to the world around us via external messages. Our families, siblings, friends, and community colored our vision of who we are today. Accurate, or inaccurate, that input became our template. As a backdrop to our self-appraisal this foundational information controls much more of our day-to-day reactions to life than we consciously imagine. These unconscious tapes lie dormant beneath the surface and are what we seek to redefine as adults. Effective at one point in time, they now need altering to allow for increased wisdom and clarity.

Parents are only able to supply the best of what they know, given their own perspective and level of awareness. In the case of information that is limiting or negative, while it may have seemed like a "truth" to our parents, caregivers, teachers or peers, it may not reflect a viewpoint that empowers us later in life. Upon that recognition we find the "groove in our tape." That thought, that concept or belief, takes on the characteristic of a scratch on a vinyl record. It distorts the clarity of an otherwise beautiful rendition of creativity and expression.

The tapes that we hear, the sentences and beliefs that lie undetected in our mind, create our outer actions and behaviors. Deeply buried in the subconscious they are the real driver behind the steering wheel. We may think we know what we want on a conscious level. We can verbally affirm our intentions, but if that directive is not in alignment with our inner tape we will never meet success in the outer world. We will never become the complete person who lives within us. The process of unearthing the truth of our unconscious belief system (our inner tapes) can initially be disturbing, but is the needed tool for removing any blockage that keeps us from achieving our dreams. Until those internal tapes are discovered, identified, and demystified, we will be living on autopilot. We will be living from the wounds of our family system, and our inherited social system. Rather than living the life we choose, life will be lived for us.

Chapter 9
Merging with our Core

In early childhood our inner tapes served as valid constructs. Though we innately found a way to maintain balance within our family system, in time we discover these unconscious tapes are confining. As adults, we can take another look at the things we hold to be our truths. We can deconstruct our limited beliefs and allow them to work for us rather than against us.

The astounding realization, in this conscious exercise, is that nothing has been lost. The faulty framework that served as our worldview and identity is actually of great benefit when deconstructed, and reconstructed properly. What was once viewed as a necessity, now begs for alteration and expansion. We begin to taste the more complete version of our own story and our newly formed thinking. In the act of unknotting the threads of our own psychological fabric we stumble upon the incredible gift those past choices provided. For every negative trait created there was a positive side it fostered.

I have a friend whose deepest desire is to have a loving, committed relationship with a partner who values her. But, she's experienced escalating versions of men who haven't honored or appreciated her. We found her hidden tape, "If I am loving and kind, attending to another person's needs and desires, then, they will love me in return." That mantra had been her childhood reality. By attending to her parents' fluctuating emotions and demands, only then, might she receive love and validation. Her default conflict— she had a core disposition of being agreeable and pleasing. She didn't believe in games, preferring to freely express loving emotions. She was on the right track to living her core truth, but off-balance. In focusing exclusively on the needs of others she never acknowledged her own feelings. That put the burden and responsibility of her feeling good in the hands of others. Learning to love ourselves is the greatest gift we can give to those we love.

We dismantled the skewed tape and found an argument she could believe. Intellectually, she agreed with the concept that we are all responsible for our own happiness. So, it wasn't a far leap to convince her that she wasn't responsible for the happiness of others as well. We began by getting her comfortable with honoring her own needs. I urged her to take a breath before automatically saying "yes" to everything asked of her. By taking the time to check in with herself first, she could make an active decision based on her own needs and desires. Her default response activated itself. She felt guilty and thought she was a "bad person" when she didn't drop everything to leap into action to comply with her boyfriend's needs. But she quickly learned that by taking care of her own needs, the shift she'd always wanted occurred.

She became aware of her feelings and chose to act out of pleasure and joy, rather than from autopilot. No longer resentful and no longer needing a reward at the end of an unwanted task, she felt happy and empowered. In less than a week her inattentive and unappreciative boyfriend surprised her at her door with flowers and food; he wanted to prepare their dinner together. He'd never been this kind of man before because she'd never been that kind of woman before. By adjusting her inner tape the balance in their relationship took a delightful new turn for both of them. He valued a woman who valued herself, while being loving and real. Both parties were now liberated to a greater design.

The trick to changing our tape is to find a manner in which a new idea agrees with our disposition. The attempt to alter a belief is useless toil if the new thought is not in alignment with our core. The core is where our power lies. If, at our core, we are loving and gentle in nature the new thought must radiate from that origin. If, at our core, we need to come from the ethical use of power we need to create new tapes that hold those tenets. Whatever are our core dispositional traits and beliefs, the new ideas and versions of readjusted thoughts must emanate from those principles or they cannot work. It's simply a question of reframing the old thought to be in agreement with our desires. Then, the implementation of those thoughts will feel natural. We will be united with ourselves. There will be no resistance or hesitation. What was once our point of pain is now our point of power. To activate the greater gift we can push through the construct of self-imposed limitation to experience the fullness of authentic expression. To give up the smaller safety of learned behavior is the beginning of self-love.

Chapter 10
Owning our Power

Why is personal power so threatening to our selves and to others? Why aim to become the finer cut of what we envision, only to feel guilty about our achievements or create roadblocks to our success? We're playing out the dictates of inner tapes that stem from a faulty framework. The early child-mind intuitively creates its own unique formula for survival: to gain love, attention, avoid conflict or minimize competition. A logical formula at the time, it served its purpose in balancing the family power base.

We've inherited a thought system with clearly defined parameters. There are two oppositional pillars of ideology from which we determine our life's narrative. Things are good or bad, right or wrong. There are winners or losers. In a black and white system of analysis, win/win isn't an option. Only recently has this concept been added to our social awareness as a valid choice. Due to its novelty, some people still carry the subliminal message that in order to attain personal power someone else will be hurt, or lose in the process. Though parental messages reinforce striving to be our best, we can still feel the need to fail in order to offset harm to others.

I have a dear friend who is bright, highly educated, and assertive. He's a born leader and a true gentleman. A visionary in business, he wanted to revitalize failing companies. He had all the makings to be an excellent captain of industry. Yet, he was floundering. Something was stopping him from realizing his true potential. We discovered the underlying tape that had repeatedly held him back from claiming his inborn greatness. That tape stated, "If I accomplish my goals I'll be competing with my father. I'll be usurping his role of alpha male and meet disapproval." True or not, this was his belief. In his family system, he inherited an unspoken "non-competition clause." Were he to succeed he'd threaten his father and therefore lose his father's love. His unconscious choice for survival came at the price of his own inner peace. Either way, he was programmed to fail.

To reconstruct his inner tape we needed to work with ideas that matched his deepest core values. We created a broader scenario by highlighting the benefits to society of his effective management. In this version of his new tape, all prosper. This narrative motivated him to move forward and cancelled out the underlying concern for eclipsing his father. He was able to manifest his desired reality without experiencing inner conflict. He bought several failing companies and re-employed all the workers who had been fired. He was empowered, and at peace.

To allow our fullest expression in this world we must allow ourselves to become the greatest version of that which we can envision. In doing so, we may upset the ego of others. But it isn't our duty to be less, in order to create a false balm of empowerment for others. We can't eliminate our finest expression to alleviate the burden of those who haven't done their inner work. We can't be less to make them feel like more.

Chapter 11
Default Mode

Inner tapes dictate habitual patterns of unconscious behavior. When we are stressed our default mode kicks into autopilot. If we are runners, we run. Procrastinators hide under the weight of their excuses and victims abdicate responsibility. We find ourselves immersed in situations that create the very reactions we protest. Tempted to blame others, we lull ourselves into a false belief that the unwanted reality is happening *to* us, rather than exacerbated *by* us.

All personal choice is eliminated when the default mode sets our course of response. We live our life's movie in repetition; our auto-default sets the stage and dictates the storyline. We find ourselves reacting to life rather than creating the life we desire. Like a novice tennis player pitted against a pro, we dart back and forth in desperation to return the object hurling over the net. We have the power to change this dynamic. If we consciously alter our habitual response we offer an opening to a new storyline with new outcomes.

Although it may seem like a daunting task to disentangle our inner tapes and core beliefs from present day behavior, the very act of becoming conscious (of this information) sets in motion a release from our unconscious. Once we can identify our core beliefs and default responses we are on the way to becoming our authentic selves.

These initial shifts in action may feel uncomfortable. But, we soon discover our new choices create new and improved scenarios. The opportunity for enhanced outcomes is liberating and thrilling. Suddenly, we realize we have limitless options when we're in the driver's seat. We are living life in the fertile present rather than the predictable past.

At some point, we get the message. We are the one constant factor in our life's movie. We're the leading character, scriptwriter, director and editor. It's tempting to blame the other actors. They weren't supposed to say those lines or walk off-stage when they did. It's easier to shift the responsibility to anyone and anything else... our parents, our partners or the world. But at the end of the day, it's just us. While that realization can be difficult, it is also the beginning of true liberation. We create our life and the story we live. We can alter it to reflect our increasing awareness. We can choose.

Chapter 12
Social Scripts

Awareness of our inner tapes allows for their dismantling. We create new tapes in correspondence to augmented knowledge. We neutralize their default mode to make pro-active choice our new reality. Yet, there lies another tier of encumbrance along the journey toward authentic living. Guaranteed to set us up for guilt and failure, it is comparative in nature. I call it our "Social Scripts."

Each socioeconomic group has its own fundamental doctrines and prescribed directives for world participation. These codes of behavior dictate the proper road to success and define our worth as a human being. Depending upon where we live, our religious upbringing and economic class, there are the established guidelines as to the "correct" form of living. These scripts contain the hidden narrative by which we judge our merit in the outer world.

I was given my script as a young girl. Even though it wasn't handed to me in writing, I knew its dictates by heart. I was to complete a specific set of tasks that would secure my conformity, and therefore my happiness. Outdated by today's standards, my script reflected the social consciousness of its time period. This blueprint silently guided my peers to their life-choices; some of them reaped great happiness from its guidance. Others remain confused as to why their perfect execution of these expectations has left them feeling empty and unfulfilled.

The scripts we inherit are neither good nor bad. It is only in determining what parts of the script we truly want, that we will rejoice in our choices. Here is the checklist of what I understood to be my assignment for successful living:

1. Be beautiful and socially adept.

Honed through private schooling, finishing schools and exposure to world travel; beauty and grace were the hallmark of women's worth. As a basic requirement a young woman had to be interesting, diverse, and shapely. Horsemanship, dancing, scholastic events, and other talents must be refined as bait for entrée to the position she would assume later in life.

2. Go to the best schools.

Preferably private, boarding, and college. College was at that time more of a status symbol than a basis for employment. It would further expand young women's exposure to successful young men.

3. Speak fluent French.

A frivolous language for an American unless one intends to live abroad or look impressive when ordering dinner.

4. Marry well.

This one was unalterable. It was the way of the world, and expected. To marry was better than not at all, but to "marry well" was the real objective. The husband must also be well bred, from a distinguished family and preferably attractive and athletic. Whether his money was inherited or he actually worked, he must be considered a "catch" in order to secure one's position as a "worthwhile female."

5. Breed beautiful children.

Beautiful blonde children were part of the accessory line of a prominent woman. A woman's day was spent at the private country club, languidly lounging in the sun while keeping one eye on her brood playing in the pool. Gin and tonic in hand, surrounded by other women who had completed this task, she would spend her afternoons recounting exciting ski trips, exotic vacations, charitable events, and local gossip.

6. Continue to be beautiful and athletic while perfecting the skills of social secretary.

As an extension of their youth, the women who were able to check off this task were the same women who, as girls, played tennis in their frilly white underpants tantalizingly exposed above lean tanned thighs. They were referred to by their nicknames such as Kiki, Missy, and Muffy. They had a mean backhand and were adept at golf as well. Now as mothers and wives in good standing they volunteered at the church or hospital, and were active in Junior League. Presentation was everything, and they understood the value of their image in their husbands' work and social life.

7. Maintain a "looking good" family.

Despite the husbands' alcoholism and philandering, well-decorated primary residences were expected and country homes were to be well managed. Gardening and landscaping were important. Entertaining was done with grace and confidence. Theme parties were a big hit and the bigger the better. But at all costs remain silent about any personal trauma and the children's drug addictions (not good social PR.) If you maintain the image, you might eventually believe it yourself.

8. Live vicariously through your husband and children, while aging gracefully.

Remain married, no matter what the cost. Impress friends and acquaintances with photos of happy grandchildren and loving, successful adult children. When beauty diminishes, perfect wit and be well dressed. You are a matron now and entitled to be blunt and caustic—finally, a true perk. You've earned it.

If you don't know your social script or are unfamiliar with the fine print, take a good look at the next situation that sends you into a tailspin. The answer lies within the problem. When knocked off balance by an event or comment, listen to the underlying message you hear as your immediate response. Words and statements come flooding to the surface in the form of self-reproach. Social expectations can be deeply layered within a series of messages that state you are faulty, have failed, or done something improperly by not making certain choices. The hot-button experience has unearthed the "should" statements in your script, making you question your worth.

There's merit in reviewing our beliefs. It means we're willing to update our thinking. We're allowing for the flow of new information to filter into our existing databank. We are evolving. If we never challenged ourselves to expand beyond our current beliefs we'd still be the same person we were in the 7th grade. I always found it amusing to see written on my yearbook, "I hope you never change."

Self-assessment and personal reflection clarify what we currently believe. In utilizing these two skills we have the ability to integrate updated concepts into our value system. There is a sharp distinction between healthy self-appraisal and external judgment. For those that seek growth and an evolving consciousness, it's wise to recognize the difference and create your own set of assignments for successful living.

Chapter 13
The Point of No Return

I remember the exact moment I knew I'd crossed the line. It was a clear, sunny, spring day in 1998. I had taken a studio apartment in Manhattan, seeking refuge from the constriction of the smaller consciousness in my given rural community. As I sat on my floral sofa during that monumental realization, the colors melted together through my tears. I had come to the point of no return. I'd left my social script years ago in search of that which was real and meaningful. In that pivotal moment, I knew that there was no going back to the sanctity of a life that was so far from the person I'd become.

I had always imagined, like the prodigal son, I would one day return to my roots. When all my exploration and alternative choices had been played out, I would again merge with my social group. I would be able to live out my given script with a peace of mind, having gotten this "thing" out of my system and delight in the reunion with a larger segment of the world. But inside, I'd gone too far beyond the world from which I came. Consciously, mentally, and philosophically, I could not return to the paradigm of my original birth. And, I cried with the unmistakable knowledge I had neither clan nor group to run to for comfort.

I'd only met a few individuals that thought as I thought, also teetering on the fringes of an unscripted life. Outside and unable to squeeze back in, I berated whatever impulses had forced my nonconformity. The point of no return wasn't met with relief but rather with self-hatred and reprimand. I didn't then understand the power of the inner spirit seeking my liberation. I hadn't made peace with discarding the parts of my assignment that no longer served me. I only knew what I had lost and could not recover.

Making peace with our true self may not reflect the social scripts we were given. Making peace with our authenticity may feel like a deliberate separation from the greater world in which we live. Until the security of the inner voice speaks more boldly than the din of the outer echoes, we will experience displacement and self-doubt. It is only the force of the spirit within that is our constant companion. That spirit seeks to be given the freedom to express its true nature by way of our life.

We may not understand the transit we're to take or the methodology by which its completion is revealed. Real freedom is won in honoring the true voice that guides us toward our greater self—not a freedom of common grouping or mass merging but ultimately a "home" within ourselves that is eternal. It's this home in which we find ourselves slowly, consistently at one with the greater masses, yet separate and real—not "a part of" prescribed thoughts and actions but part of a collective that touches the higher thought and clearer perspective of those around us. It is this home of internal awareness that allows an ongoing merging with the greater social system. And in the end, as we truly merge with our authentic selves we begin to delight in the knowledge that wherever we are, we are home.

PART THREE
Through the Eye of the Needle

Chapter 14
Everything Happens for a Reason, and Why

"Everything happens for a reason." This saying has reached epic proportions as a "catch all" commentary for all things mysterious that can't be explained. Routinely stated with confident conviction this phrase is the acknowledgement of unknown factors crafting a rationale that is apparent, but not understood. The person who utters this statement is clearly commenting on the presence of a design that exists. What that design is, and what it intends, are the unanswered second half of this incomplete statement.

"Everything happens for a reason" serves as a partial explanation to an event that is serendipitous, or unusual. Rarely is this phrase used when a divorce is eminent or a diagnosis of cancer has been given. "Everything," means everything. It can't include some good things and exclude unwanted things. If one were to truly believe everything happens for a reason, then all situations apply.

Things happen for intended reasons. Desired or undesired, all occurrences have their explicit reasons. To find the answer as to "why" everything happens, we need to know how to read the architecture of the situation presented. Within it, lie the answers we seek. Otherwise, it's simply an excuse for that which we haven't yet identified.

Reading the architecture of life requires looking for the clues. What is trying to occur? What are the greater reasons for such an occurrence? What connections are seeking to be made and what is their elevated purpose for all involved? What is dying, and what is seeking to be born from that death? When we begin to identify the road signs we begin to see the route we are being asked to take. When we note the patterns we begin to see the overview of the ultimate journey. The greater design occurring is supreme in its efforts and relentless in its application.

Deciphering the information within its vehicle of presentation is a skill that can be refined. It isn't difficult. But it does take a different mentality to decode the message in the occurrence. It requires a looking through, and looking beyond the physical appearance of any given situation. It takes an eagle's perspective, as the human embraces the emotions of the event and the observer witnesses the all-encompassing transaction of that which occurs. It is the combination of both participant and observer that activate the keen awareness of "why things happen."

All events, situations and people are merely vehicles to our advancement. That advancement is the advancement of our soul's understanding of our higher purpose in this physical life experience. The physical experience is only an illusion. The true reality of our participation here is far greater. Physical reality is our playing field. It's the place we come to work things out and to learn new ways of being as we refine the vision of who we are to become.

Chapter 15
The Process of Personal Evolution

Personal evolution is contingent upon a willingness to change and grow. It requires allowing for a state of flux. Until new behavioral attitudes become dominant we must accept moments of chaos—the unknown. This process of evolving requires a sense of curiosity and adventure. Evolution is natural. It is the birth of new information that later becomes old information. It is fluid. The only constant factor in this process is change.

Personal evolution requires self-knowledge and self-awareness. We become the "observer" as we take the eagle's perspective. When things appear to be in crisis, the eagle's perspective can see the total picture. We can observe the actions of others with greater clarity from this all-encompassing, yet detached, state. Our need to be in control, right, or have our ego satisfied becomes a non-issue. Suddenly, we can see the entire transaction with a sense of awe. People are doing what they know in a manner familiar to them: sometimes well, and at other times based on limited choices. Each person is playing out his or her own level of awareness. Correspondingly, when the entire viewpoint has shifted the summation of what has occurred shifts in response.

Seeing the greater architecture of life enables release from our struggles and the attainment of true freedom. Understanding the process IS the tool. Inner tapes are dismantled and reframed in accordance with our inner truth. The default mode is neutralized in our acting from conscious choice. Our social scripts are observed and altered to serve us, allowing our ability to flourish without constraint. Life becomes rich and rewarding. We're finally living the truth that lies in our heart and demonstrating its power to the world.

We discover a sense of flow. The natural rhythm of life is moving us from one desire to the next, and from each new understanding to the apex of its expression. There is a sense of smoothness and structure to all that is occurring. We begin to see the outlines of a pattern of assistance. In recognizing the terrain, we now move swiftly through each passage in anticipation of the gifts that lie ahead. No longer a victim of life's mysteries we become an acutely aware participant in this perfectly crafted vehicle of expansion.

Chapter 16
The Cycles of Life

Life offers us an astounding architecture by which to understand the cycles of our own life. The clues are inherent in the physical world. Nature has its seasons. The tides flow in and out. After day, there is nightfall. The animal kingdom reverently obeys its own cycles. Yet, we as humans seek to focus only on those segments we "prefer" to experience, not understanding that the numerous forms of "death" we experience are an integral part of the expansion process.

There is a continuum to all the minor deaths and births that occur within our lives. We expand beyond where we were, to enter a new awareness. In the obvious occurrence of these transitions we often fail to honor the patterns of our own cycles when presented with the opportunity to do so. We fight to maintain our current position when we are pressed to advance. We look at endings as finalities, rather than seeing them as a new emergence. Making peace with these cycles is the key to true freedom. A willingness to experience the totality of life without argument is the glory of living fully.

Consciously or unconsciously, growth is what humans are striving toward. And yet, we resist change due to our need for security. So herein lies the conflict. We're born into a world we don't fully understand. We create constructs of beliefs to stabilize our transit. We search for answers, busy ourselves with minutiae to avoid asking key questions, or numb-out in our preference for accepting the scripts and stories we've been given. Seeking some form of stability to manage the events that occur, we often fail to notice the overall architecture of assistance provided by each of these death and rebirth cycles. They cradle our voyage to each new transition. These cycles are the vehicle by which we move through our lives to augmented positions of understanding and action, while unaware of the repetitive patterns of their presentation.

This is the method of human evolution: an ongoing series of births, deaths, and the promise of a new beginning. It is our path to learning. This amazing design within our life experience is trying in all ways, and at all times, to assist us. But we resist. In our limited thinking, we protest those things we feel are not progressing, as they should. We miss the cycles. We don't see the greater design or its intention. We defer to anxiety and stress instead of trust and flow. We dig deeper, add more resolve and press for our version of what life "should" provide. Yet, behind the veiled curtain, there is a fortune awaiting our acceptance.

Then comes a moment when all our learned techniques fail. The tried and true methods that rendered us the specific results we wanted, no longer work. When that stunningly odd day comes we begin the frantic shuffle: the hunt and search for reconfiguration. We try in desperation to repeat known methodologies. We infuse more conviction. We redouble our efforts. But still, we're hopelessly lost in a state of confusion. How do we begin the reconstruction? Why is it that what once worked, now fails us?

The death cycle comes for one reason only—to pry our hands loose of that to which we stubbornly cling. A greater gift is on the horizon. Death is the beginning of the birth cycle but it reveals itself in a cloaked manner. It's the end of all we know and all we are, up to that point in time. It's the onslaught of doors that slam in our face. It's the application of all known, tried and true efforts that no longer yield results. The death cycle doesn't win any popularity contests. It's arduous, painful, and exhausting when viewed in short sight. But, from an expanded perspective we can understand that its purpose is to liberate us.

Chapter 17
Death Cycle at 2 am

My friend experienced his own death cycle one pivotal evening in 2005. Having chronic panic attacks, anxiety, and depression resulting from 30 years of drug and alcohol abuse he finally hit his "meltdown" phase. High on drugs and alcohol since his Bar Mitzvah, Maurizio had used these coping methods to manage the insecurities of adolescence and adulthood.

I'd met Maurizio a year earlier through mutual friends. He was cultured, entertaining and had a great sense of humor. Speaking six languages and having lived all over the world, he was an immediate party favor. Whenever Maurizio showed up the festivities began. As a casual acquaintance I enjoyed him, as did scores of others. Possessing a sunny disposition without malice, this man was an interesting mixture of intelligence and warmth. Oddly, the drugs and alcohol that he thought made him more interesting were tolerated only due to the fact that he was such a great guy.

That night, Maurizio had accidently terrorized my local deli owner while trying to buy more beer to offset his frenzy. Holding a beer bottle (of his own) with one hand under his shirt, Maurizio placed a 6-pack on the counter with twenty-dollar bill. Mistaking the beer bottle under Maurizio's shirt for a gun, the attendant waved off the cash off with panic stricken eyes, "No. No. All okay. Take!! Take!!" Not fully realizing what had happened, Maurizio kept insisting to pay. The deli owner refused to relent and threw Maurizio's twenty-dollar bill in the shopping bag with his beer.

All cycles must come to an end. Normally, we aren't subject to these private moments. Known for writing until late into the morning hours, I was awake and available to witness the miracle as it unfolded in front of my eyes that night. Maurizio sought the only person he knew who was coherent at 2 am. With a free 6-pack and single beer, Maurizio came to my home. He recalls the night he lapsed into his profound death cycle.

I'd reached the end of my rope. Anxious, scared and with no one else to turn to, Susan was my last stop. I was considering going to the hospital. I didn't know what to do. She told me every thing's going to be okay—which is the last thing I wanted to hear. And, that it's actually very good what's happening—which was even less of what I wanted to hear. I thought maybe I came to the wrong place but I had nowhere else to go. Is everybody crazy? She's not getting what I'm telling her. And, she's smiling... which is pissing me off. I'm on my 4th beer, ranting and going on about the horrors of my life. But now I'm more relaxed so I can actually listen to what she has to say. She tells me that this is the end, and calls it a "death cycle." She's using these words like "rebirth" and "positive." Okay I'm calm due to the booze. So then I heard it, slightly. While it looks very bad it's really good. I'd sunk to my lowest level but I put on a brave face. I felt she was coming from a good place and was trying to help me but maybe she was a little misguided. What I needed from her was compassion, and, "don't worry honey." But she was laughing and happy. I thought she was reveling in my misery. She let me crash on the sofa. When I woke up the next day, I knew I needed help. Hung over, anxious, and unfocused, I knew I had to do something about it.

Maurizio, NYC

When we know the cycles we can see the next step to be taken. What is feared to be our "ending" is actually our "beginning." Maurizio gained his sobriety and got a new life. While appearing happy isn't what a friend wants to see from us in the moment of their own personal death, the knowledge of their next transit is clear to those of us who understand these cycles.

It isn't the death cycle that will take us down. It's the lack of awareness as to the reason for that death that is our torment. The death cycle clears the way for a new birth. There are times the fields must be burned completely to allow for vibrant new growth. The death cycle activates our next incarnation, while we are living. Knowledge of the greater purpose of these cycles is the balm that alleviates the pain of transit.

Chapter 18
Tuck and Roll

When the death cycle begins, tuck and roll. Trust me on this one. Just go with it because you can't hang on to what is imploring to be released. The longer you hang on to the known the longer it takes to get to the new destination, and the more you'll be battered in the process. When the shift happens there is a choice to resist or accept. Let the current take you. Yes, it can be terrifyingly uncomfortable. There are no recognizable markers and no guideposts. You've been catapulted to a new terrain and a new reality. There is, however, ample guidance to support you. It may come in forms to which you are unaccustomed or from individuals you would have formerly dismissed. There are no coincidences. Pay attention. All of life is speaking to you in every opportunity presented.

The tricky part is allowing the death cycle to perform its job. No matter how badly the old situation or former life appeared, it came with hopes and dreams. The loss of a dream eclipses the smaller characters and events contained therein. Even if the former cycle was resplendent with promise, there comes the time that all things must change. In theory, recognition of a death cycle should make the transit easier. But as human beings we cling to the need for control. We've been trained from birth to seek structure and definition. From our smaller vision a loss is still registered as a loss—even if the old life or situation was something we prayed to eliminate. Each time one of these death cycles hit, the tendency is to force life to conform to our wishes. More control, bargaining, negotiating, and readjustment. Maybe just a miracle or two. But the death cycle won't budge. Nothing works and nothing will work. All the doors close and there is only an empty space in which we face our unknown future.

It's been my observation that as one becomes more conscious of these cycles, the cycles quicken. The duration time between death and birth cycles contracts. Recognition of the process (seeing it for what it really is) allows for fluid transit. Again, this all sounds good in theory. Intellectual understanding and emotional reaction are two entirely different things. Each cycle has its specific dynamics and set of challenges. Some cycles are easier than others. There are cycles designed to shake us to the core, demanding the release of an entire way of being and/or thinking. Giving up and surrendering are concepts that go against the codes of survival, yet in this case they are the antidotes for the malady.

For the record let me honestly state that I have kicked, bucked, and sobbed my way through much of this process. Not every time, but many times. Even though I know the pattern in advance and know that a true improvement follows the death cycle, the human need for security and resolution has tested me on every level. Able to watch myself as both participant and observer, I see a woman stubbornly clinging to the lesser while knowing the greater is possible. Then the nutty thinking starts. What if the Universe gives me less? How will I know "the new" will be better? Procrastinating under the exit sign, I try to convince myself to open the door to the unknown. Maybe I left something behind? Oh, who cares. I'm so exhausted it doesn't matter. Then comes the final kick in the butt of more pain. And amazingly, I'm willing. But there's a gap. It's the Void: the space in between one door closing and another opening. It's the nothingness before the shift occurs. I can't go back but I'm not yet moving forward. The void is the temporary pause between total surrender and faith-filled acceptance.

Life is like a doggie agility course. The dog trots through tunnels, leaps over fences and jumps through hoops. It takes practice. At first the tunnels are daunting; so dark and strange. But with their masters' encouragement they continue onward to discover light on the other side of the tunnel, and a clearing. Fences look intimidating. They're so high. They appear to be barriers... and just like those doggies we find ourselves between what we can see in front of us, and what lies beyond the horizon of our current knowledge. And, the hoops. They're really just for show. But in some circles, presentation is everything.

My take on this: the faster I can get through life's agility course the sooner I'll arrive at the next adventure. As I confront life's transits, the attending levels of understanding come more easily. Ah. More compliance. Greater trust. It's the system of movement and the benevolent architecture of design that quickens my advancement. As I think of the doggie agility course, I know there is a treat awaiting my effort.

Chapter 19
Jump-starting The Cycle

There are times when we feel stalled. Nothing seems to be moving forward. At least in the death cycle there's movement toward a definitive ending. I've been stuck in-between careers and in-between important life-choices. One way to jump-start a stagnant cycle is to begin to close the doors voluntarily. This can be done in a multitude of ways. By slamming the door shut on areas that no longer work we allow an opening for new opportunities to emerge. The shutting of doors can take the form of eliminating negative friends, cleaning out closets, or purging negative/outdated thoughts.

I have a friend who is academically, scary-smart. As an American woman she chose to become fluent in French for reasons beyond looking refined at dinner. Sally translates analytical treatises. She's a researcher, documentary filmmaker and on the board of dozens of prestigious women's organizations. Anxious to begin a new project, we began brainstorming for new ideas. With so many options, where to begin? I suggested she note where her passion lies. What was the thing that gave her goose bumps? What subject ignited her interest? With that observation in mind, I asked her to close the doors to all things to the contrary that drained her vitality and spirit.

When stalled, the process of remnant elimination can move a stagnant situation forward. There are always things that can be released. There are thoughts, jobs, obligations, and people no longer in concert with us that can be eliminated. There's a saying; "The Universe hates a vacuum." In actively taking the initiative into our own hands, we can jump-start any cycle we find in stasis.

Busy-ness, isn't productivity. It feels like movement, yet it has no focus. Staying busy and over-obligated to organizations/people and situations that don't resonate with us is an exercise in circular movement. No forward acceleration is created. If you find yourself wanting to jump-start a new cycle, begin by re-evaluating the things to which you have committed your time and energy. Is all of this activity necessary? We are under the false impression that outer actions create gainful advancement. Not so. Outer actions without inner clarity and focus are useless toil. Ten minutes spent on inner reflection will reap greater results than twenty hours of agitated outer actions lacking clarity and purpose.

We may not see where we are headed. We may not know the job title or career avenue we seek in which to best express ourselves. We may not see the outline of the new partnership we desire or the new life we seek to create. But, we can identify the qualities we want to experience within those constructs. In doing that, we are focused and headed toward our desire with clarity. Do we want a job that will serve a greater good, feel meaningful, imbued with mutual respect and wise usage of our talents? Do we want a partnership that promotes genuine, honest, growth-oriented love? Do we want to create a lifestyle that will allow us to be productive while also having time to enjoy our friends and family? In gaining clarity on the qualities we want to experience within the new cycle, we will summon all corresponding and cooperative forces to us. We will draw to us that which we desire in content.

That clarity allows an opening for the manifestation of our dreams to occur in numerous forms of presentation. We are neither limiting nor outlining the manner of their presentation, or how they must occur. We are creating the foundation from which the perfect vehicle may come to us, without resistance and without detailing the fine points of its form. Open to all opportunities and situations that match our desire, we may now relax in the knowledge that we've done our work. As greater clarity comes, we refine our vision. Situations present themselves. People show up in our lives unexpectedly. We discover we are working in another format, with a force that seeks to align us with our greatest wishes.

Chapter 20
The Void

The empty spot between death and birth is what I call the Void. It is stillness—the place of no movement. It's the gap between these two cycles where all feels frozen in nothingness. The void is the point of transition where the seeds of new growth have taken root, yet no sign of bloom is presented. In opposition to the thrashing turbulence of the death cycle that seeks to loosen our grip on that which is no longer of service, the void feels stark by comparison. As the image of a vast desert, bleak and colorless, the absence of emotion is a welcome respite. Not high and not low, but a flat line without extremes. The stillness marks the transition of the old life dying and a new passage to the greater experience emerging.

When in the void cycle, to exert effort is a pointless act. This is the place of rest and the place of faith. Life is taking us somewhere unexpected. The best way I've found to deal with this phase is to allow it to perform its inherent miracle. To allow for the birth of the unknown is both marvelous and terrifying. That's why faith is a requisite. The architecture of life knows the next step for us and will dutifully provide our transitional opportunities. The void is not stagnation. Whereas stagnation may require a jump-start to prompt closure of a death cycle, the void is the completion of the death cycle. All has ended. All doors have been closed, and emptiness is the only attending emotion. The struggle is clearly over. The void simply asks for our patience.

Think of it as a shifting of gears. The gears are big, and must settle completely before re-calibration. We are not taught to see the value of stillness. Our world doctrine values effort and the achievement one's goals. It is this belief system that activates our resistance to the void, and pre-empts this cycle from allowing us the needed time to gain our internal stability. The more we can become aware of the nature of these cycles the more we can allow their coming and going, moving easily without resistance.

Management of growth cycles require different tools than those taught to us by the world. We are dealing with two entirely different sets of constructs. And here, the worldview fails to provide valuable input as to these transitions. Goals in the world necessitate focus, discipline, and persistence. Human evolution requires awareness, trust, and surrender. They are the dictates of nature, and nature will not conform to the dictates of man.

To wait in the emptiness is to wait upon instruction. The instructions come from navigating within oneself and assessing re-calibration in light of what has been learned by the tearing away of the death cycles. It's in the personal re-adjustment that the focus can be placed. In the time where no outward movement exists, internal shifts create a focal point for work to be done. The shift can be a mental construct, a known way of behavior, or simply an inner listening with deeper connection to the voice of the true self.

The void heralds a time of reconnecting with the self, as all things outer cease to detour our attention. There is a natural urging toward solitude. While it may *appear* as withdrawal in response to the chaotic forces of the former death cycle, it isn't retreat. The void holds a rich sweetness in its separation from external activity. Though appearing as separation, it's inwardly a time of gathering. It's the rest after a long journey that reflects upon all that has been gained in the appearance of that which seems lost.

I have noted well the human characteristic of impatience, in myself. Knowing the brevity of this life I want to move quickly through each stage of each cycle. But this is exactly where I have to submit to a system far wiser than myself. My only job is to trust the process. My only action is to go with it. To resist, creates a slowing of the underlying movement. Fighting guarantees prolonged anxiety, not advancement.

How long does the void cycle last? It depends upon the level of resistance. I've gotten through it in a day, and I've had it last for weeks. But, when in doubt, I suggest the following: Do the opposite of all you've been told. When life has told you to fight and leap into action, relax and play. When life has instructed you to push and control, ease up and let go. Do anything that isn't in the script, and you'll come out ahead. I remember one void cycle where I felt urged to watch American TV. Any TV show, no matter how awful. I simply chalked that up to too much time living abroad, where my only connection to life in America was re-runs of *Hercules* dubbed in Spanish.

There are times we feel the inner shift has clearly occurred, yet the outer forces feel slow to respond. There is a reason. Actually, there are many reasons. Some we will discover, others we will not. The point is to continue ahead with the individual work that we can do and utilize that as our method of being proactive. And, relax. Allow the void to take you to where you are headed. Let life guide you to the birth of who you are becoming. The merging of inner and outer forces will come together. Beautifully.

PART FOUR
Initiation

Chapter 21
Ugly Duckling

There is a part of the birth cycle that I call the "Ugly Duckling" phase. It's when the death cycle has occurred, the void has passed, and the newborn emerges. Noted for its awkwardness, one is thrust into the discomfort of infancy as an adult. My first experience with this phase was met with shame, fear, and confusion. It was excruciating for me not to be "looking good" in the eyes of colleagues and the outside world—a young woman thrashing about in search of her bearings. Not esteemed socially or professionally, the experience of a newborn with wobbly legs attempting to function in a fast-paced world is humbling. Smooth and graceful seem beautiful, disoriented and unsure don't. But this ugly duckling is actually a thing of greater splendor than its former image. It is the sign of re-birth to a new life. There are footsteps never before taken and thoughts never before activated. Yet, this phase is beautiful as a momentary marker of what one is to become.

The ugly duckling stage never seems to happen at an appropriate time. The first big death toward rebirth comes from its own volition. Like molting, or the skin being shed by a snake, it has its own time and season. Though the former polished life may have a remnant splurge of activity, it's closer to the 4 am crowd leaving a bar: disheveled and woozy.

I was in college when I first experienced the peculiar nature of this phase. I studied voice. I never loved opera but I went to a great music school where that was the only game in town. Like most young singers in their late teens/early twenties, I had an image of what a classically trained voice should sound like. I imitated the famous singers that I admired: Renata Tibaldi, Mirella Freni, Renata Scotto, and Kiri Te Kanawa. My young voice didn't have the depth of the idols; they were 15-20 years my senior. In my desire to sound like the diva I wasn't, I developed a "cover." I thought I sounded pretty good until I switched teachers and the new vocal coach required me to quit covering my real voice. He argued that the most beautiful voice was my "true voice." He insisted that finding our true voice was something unique to us, and its singular beauty belonged to no one else. He coached me through the terrifying process of letting go of the former sounds I'd thought were of greater worth than my own authentic voice.

My practice room had a small window. People could look in as they passed by the room. I covered it with paper out of humiliation for the horrible sounds I was making. Since I could no longer cover my voice, I could at least cover the window. My voice was unwieldy. It lacked depth. It was uncoordinated and raw. I felt like an ugly duckling. I made noises that were (to my ears) ugly and unrefined. But something in my teacher's words resonated as being true. I decided since I had beaten my head against the wall trying to be somebody other than myself, I would now try to find my true voice. I stayed with this process. Eventually I caught glimpses of my natural voice, which was surprisingly more interesting than my meager attempt at imitation.

Sometimes life offers us "Previews of Coming Attractions." I use that term for events/situations experienced at one point in time, that foreshadow their greater significance at a later date. All of us are in the midst of our own evolutionary continuum. When we can match the patterns and connect the dots within these previews, we can incorporate the information to assist us in the next leg of our journey. Although I had a preview of this transit in one aspect of my life, I was unprepared for its reoccurrence some 10 years later. The next event that fell into this pattern was when my "cover" took the form of my socially acceptable identity, rather than my voice.

I was living in Manhattan. I had a respectable career, long-term boyfriend, and a nice apartment on the Upper West Side. I was following an allowable variation of my social script. My exterior image presented well, yet underneath the smooth surface lurked a shifting foundation. I was following the instructions, but missing the most essential component: me living *my* life. I soon found myself in a massive death cycle brought about by a series of escalating events. My father died, my company folded, I left a 10-year relationship, and watched in horror as dozens of other security systems dissolved with each passing week. I applied all my well-honed techniques in a desperate attempt to put the scattered pieces back together, but to no avail. Whatever vehicle used to get me from point A to point B, now failed. Hitting a definitive wall in every aspect of my life, I knew I needed to change course. As my outer "cover" crumbled, I once again sought to find my true voice in the world.

I left the world of external power and began an inner journey. I built a home in rural northwestern New Jersey. I didn't bother to connect my television for 3 years, and canceled my subscription to the Wall Street Journal. Pop culture and world events survived without me. I spent the next decade journaling, meditating and attending workshops. I re-entered therapy and began working on issues long ignored. I learned to identify my feelings. Consciously entering the fault line that had rocked my foundational reality, I dismantled my inner tapes. I began looking at the social blueprints I'd been handed and reevaluated my goals. Instead of noting my reflection via an outer world, I discovered the power and freedom of living my truth.

Chapter 22
Forced Metamorphosis

When the "cover" was ripped off my image as an adult, this "looking good" woman entered a world for which she had no manual. Single and exploring life in a manner that resonated with me, I found myself in two back-to-back long-term relationships with much younger men. While this type of partnership model may seem irrelevant now, given the time period and location it was deemed scandalous. In a highly conservative golf course community isolated from big city thinking and alternative life choices an older woman living with younger boyfriend was not a "script" that was understood. I no longer had golf partners willing to play with me. Gone were the former invitations to house parties. And, gone were the friendly faces that had welcomed my presence.

I was again the ugly duckling, amplified. It was a sensation I remembered well. Having been the assured woman with a briefcase and a camel's hair coat, I was entering a dimension of self-discovery for which I had no point of reference. I had to be willing to give up the socially acceptable Susan, to become the new Susan. Closing the door to most of my former life, I walked into the unknown. I had no allies. I couldn't look to my newfound community for support and had few friends who understood this journey. I could only look within and keep my faith.

Though they exiled me, my immediate neighbors did so with a gracious sense of social decorum. In the outlying townships, this skill was neither endorsed nor practiced. Rumors of witchcraft spread like wildfire. How else could one explain a younger man in love with an older woman? The simple act of buying groceries or getting gas was met with dirty looks, cautious distain or outright vengeance. A local tow-truck man left me stranded on a desolate road, running in fear that I would cast a spell over his family. While the absurdity of this event is laughable to me now, I wasn't laughing when his truck pulled away leaving me alone on that barren road. As the rumors of my committing "witchcraft" escalated, I found myself called into the offices of the local cable distributor. I had a show on spirituality and higher consciousness that aired throughout the Tri-State area. The directors of this station outlet had received a petition of over 100 signatures demanding the removal of my show, to protect the welfare of the local viewers. Incomprehensibly, these events occurred one hour outside of Manhattan at the end of the twentieth century. Despite the extremity of these measures, I refused to allow aggressive ignorance force me into a compliance of undesired conformity; I refused to give up my younger boyfriend.

I never anticipated this private experience would later become the catalyst for a larger social conversation. I couldn't foresee that the destruction of my professional/social identity would propel me to a new career, and give me a new voice. I couldn't foresee writing a book nor could I envision the varied platforms by which I would be advocating for love's greater inclusion, and the broader understanding of emerging partnership models. All these future scenarios were withheld from my vision as I lived within the painful confines of my current reality. How could I possibly imagine that the very thing, for which I was reviled, would later become the same thing for which I would be lauded?

In our transit to a monumental new birth, we often lack the ability to foresee our future destination. This is especially true when the destination isn't on our life-map. We know what we're leaving. We know what we're losing. And, we know the price we are paying within that process. Rarely can we see the architectural design of where we're headed, or the magnitude of the gifts that await us. Big deaths create big shifts. Those shifts create the monumental force for our tremendous, new birth.

One of the many benefits that I reaped from my experience of character defamation was to eliminate social acceptance as a tool for self-validation. I didn't fit into "their" world, so I became the sole member of "my" new world. It was lonely at first. As I slowly adjusted to authentic living, free of shame and justification, the tenets of my former thinking began to loosen their grip on my mind. I discovered a new strength in the person I had become. No longer held to a system I never wanted in the first place, I began to taste the exquisite joy of living my own life. Fully, boldly and without apology, I continued my course. I began to trust my own dictates rather than those I had resisted, yet held to be "the right way." This ugly duckling had learned to use her wings.

Now, even in the darkest moments I am able to read the architecture of life's greater request and see the higher purpose of where it's taking me. To acquire the skill of deciphering the signposts to unknown destinations, I had to go through many deaths and births. Though I now possess this skill, it is still the human who must withstand the transit. I may choose to rail in protestation of my desired preference or move willingly with resolve. Either way, I know advancing forward is the only course of action that will summon a greater outcome.

Chapter 23
The Power of Alchemy

What we don't understand will cause our suffering. I needed to fortify my inner resolve to manage the onslaught of the daily dramas I encountered in my rural community. But I was ill equipped in that time period. I didn't have the tools I needed for the severity of the challenges I was facing. I hadn't yet identified the cycles of life, so I didn't know I was in a death phase. I couldn't see the workings of an ongoing architecture of assistance. I didn't know how to read the meaning of events beyond their appearance. Due to that lack of understanding, I was burdened with the overwhelming pain of a world crashing in on me, as I viewed each participant's delight in his or her personal contribution to my destruction.

I had but one shred of wisdom to support my sanity and give me hope: I understood alchemy. I knew that events this extreme had to have a greater purpose. Situations bearing this level of intensity don't come to destroy us for folly. They are the catalytic foundation to create alchemy. It was that sole fragment of knowledge that turned my death into a new life, as I held on to the belief that time would give me the answers I needed to transform the effects of this crisis into its intended greatness. My job was to look beyond the pain, beyond the situation, and dig for the gold within the apparent chaos.

When we experience a crisis of dramatic proportions, we can become numb to any form of thinking beyond the problem itself. We can't begin to imagine liberation within the chaos, or birth within our own destruction. We assume life has no justice and that our current crisis has no reasonable benefit. We assume the events are only what they appear to be; random and unnecessary vehicles of pain, confusion, and loss. Until we understand the power of alchemy, we assume all of this to be true.

Alchemy was a scientific, chemical venture pursued by numerous ancient cultures. Alchemists endeavored to transform base metals into gold and other noble properties. The practice of alchemy inspired a broader philosophical tenet: there exists the possibility of transforming "what is," into "what is greater." Modern day spiritual schools of thought extend the concept of alchemy to the practice of transmuting negative into positive. The energetic charge created by that act commands sovereignty over its original components.

We too, can activate this form of thinking to aid our transit through painful events and moments of personal crisis. Our perception of life is shrouded by false images and illusions of our own "perceived" reality. Metaphysics and spiritual disciplines teach us that we can transform our current reality into a greater, future realization. It's just a matter of seeing things differently. It's not our fault that we don't understand this concept when looking at life from the standpoint of "reality." Reality *appears to be* the facts of the events in question. From that position we can only assess the first layer of meaning. Reality is merely the event, itself. Living in a physical world, we tend to focus on the puppet show that's moving in front our eyes, rather than looking to the origins of these movements. The actions that occur in our physical reality command our complete attention, and that focal point creates assumptions about what we are seeing.

When confronted with a crisis or merely a situation not to our liking, we automatically call it "bad." We fail to see that the situation we label as "bad," is also the situation that carries the greatest potential for alchemy. The worse the situation = the higher the energetic charge when transformed. The greater the degree to which we unlock our thinking, the greater the amount of gold we can extract from a negative situation. This type of thinking is needed in a massive death cycle, and in all events that appear as a crisis.

There are specific steps that need to be taken to create alchemy. The first is to be willing to consider the possibility that there is a mislabeling going on, and that the "bad situation" is only a "situation." Regardless of its severity, there may be something miraculous that lies beyond our immediate comprehension. We live in a fully dimensional world. Every coin has its reverse side. Day greets night as light illuminates the dark. Would it really be too great a leap to consider another side to what we assume as "bad?" The Universe doesn't randomly torture us for fun. If we have a willingness to look at the situation differently, we have the ability to alter its outcome. We may then allow for the possibility that the conflict in question not only has a reason, but also an equal valuation based upon its potency. To the exact proportion that the situation seems negative, it has the equal degree of charge to become positive. Similar to harnessing a volt of electricity and redirecting the current, we are able to alter the apparent conflict to serve us.

This is how we can apply the power of alchemy to our day-to-day lives. Usage of this form of thinking is the key to actualizing the greater design. We can turn the worst situation into the greatest situation by looking for the blessing and the miracle within the tragedy. Each situation in life is just a situation. It's a collection of facts. No matter how horrible the event may seem to us and how destructive its facts, it's what we make those facts and events mean to us that either destroy or liberate us. One slight mental shift can alter our entire reality. One change in thought can change a hundred little consequences.

Chapter 24
Digging for Gold

Uncovering the gold hidden in life's challenges is an acquired skill. We can choose to nurture our wounds, or transform them. We can either let our past dictate our future, or we can live in the bounteous present. Philosophical alchemy asks us to look for the gift in each difficult occurrence. Instead of viewing our situation through the lens of pain, we focus on its instruction. Not to be proactive in this matter requires re-experiencing the same pain in perpetuity, via repeated patterns. Replayed to spur our acknowledgement, each reenactment bears more pressure. The increased intensity insists upon detection; it can't be ignored or repressed. Although the temptation is to pray for an external shift, the outer world won't budge until there's a shift in our inner world.

Nothing will be understood as a vehicle for greater good, if the techniques for finding the greater good remain a mystery. We will remain harnessed to our wounds. Paralyzed by not knowing the "why" of a situation that appears as "bad," the wound is in constant need of dressing. Never extracted, buried deeply or lying vulnerable to exposure, the wound continues to disable us. In reoccurring situations it makes itself known via victimization, defensiveness, and reactivity. We'll continue to wear the scar of its cut. The language we use to describe this wound is the very method of its healing. The narrative we cling to as our story, can become the story that liberates us. The thing we are losing, the thing we are wanting, and the thing we can't have is the very thing we will instead receive.

Digging for gold is the awareness that this wound indicates the exact point of power we are seeking in the outer realm. Within the cut, within the depth of its descent, we have the same proportional ability to heal and ascend. This is where "looking again" and "seeing beyond" becomes our medicine. By holding a mirror to the affliction we see its reverse image. In Open Thinking, we actualize its potency. The object that appears as pain is our gold. The ability to look at the wound again with a greater sense of vision edifies our perspective. That vision sees purpose in all that happens, and meaning in all that occurs. Nothing is random or pointless. Whatever label we give our "pain" or "wound," it is here to foster the emergence of its opposite.

The need to eliminate pain demands our attention, and our action. Pain is the voice that will always be heard and the call that must always be answered. It's one of the great tools utilized by life to activate our forward movement.

The nature of our gift, our gold, is that which appears to be withheld from us in the outer world. If approval and recognition are being torn from us, then they are what have come to be awakened. If it is love, or the assumed need of another to bring us any outer feeling of worthiness, then these are the very feelings we will access from within. If it is trust that has been violated, then it is the blessing of self-assurance and ability to trust oneself that will be gained. If it is victimization, then our course in life is one of personal empowerment. Whatever the wound, whatever the name, pain provides the method of transit to the creation of its opposite. The pain we're given is the thing we are here to transform. It is the clue to our life's purpose and possesses within it the greatest power we own.

Chapter 25
Red Warning Light

One hot, humid day I decided to drive to the beach. During the four-hour drive, my air-conditioning was blasting. I didn't notice the red engine warning light as the sun was glaring through the windows. When I finally saw it at dusk, I chose to ignore it. This was a new car. I chalked it up to the heat of the day. I assumed all was well. Wrong. I had no water. After a decade of living in New York City, a place where taxis and subways are the mode of transit, I'd forgotten some of the basics of car maintenance.

Reactivity and resistance are our emotional red warning lights. Like the lights in a car, these red lights require our immediate attention. They're triggered by inner tapes, social scripts, and limited thinking. Whenever we find ourselves upset by outer situations, it's our cue to initiate a diagnostic check. We need to dig further into ourselves to find the gift beyond what *appears to be,* and check the connections under our own hood. Could the need for our outcome be a smaller version than the intended purpose of this event? By defiantly resisting what's happening in the outer world, we're denying ourselves the possibility of a greater occurrence.

Whenever I notice my own red warning light, I refer to my owner's manual. Not to be confused with the generic factory version in the glove compartment that nobody reads—but my own manual. It has the exact information I need to deconstruct the nature of my problem.

When working off the generic manual, the actualization of all desire lies outside of ourselves. The ridiculousness of this construct is glaring in its absurdity. Self-worth is derived from the least effective sources: other people and external events. Not predictable, not controllable, and not our business. Twisting outer events and people to conform to our needs is exhausting. Bad odds, and rarely possible. The act of exerting this type of ongoing effort negates the joy of living. Happiness is forever out of reach, or if attained in the temporal, is fleeting. Stress, worry, anxiety, fear, and all other variations of discontent perpetually haunt us. The feelings of being powerless, victimized, and struggling aren't synonymous with the joy of living.

The need to have a specific outcome is rarely an authentic need. It's inherited from the greater social blueprint that contains the definitions of success/failure, win/loss, and all scenarios that equate our position on the game board of self-worth. Its information has been ingrained into our thinking from birth. Therefore, it takes a concerted effort to dismantle this method for measuring our self-worth.

What do we really know? Are we certain that what "we want" is really the best for us? Only now am I learning the ease and joy of trusting life to work with me, and for me. The key to shifting my perspective lies in seeking what I think I need in the outer world and building it within myself. Then I have a shot at living fully.

A life lived fully is an experience that happens when we allow space for the magic to occur. In the span of that gap, the miraculous can prevail over the known. It is in the act of choosing trust over the anxiety of self-will that life is able to produce its miracle. It takes vigilance to remind oneself that the root of all discontent is control. Control is a lack of faith in the architecture of assistance. Trust is the choice to defer to a superior wisdom. Choosing to act on trust, rather than control, is the application of knowledge gained by observing the brilliance of the force that seeks our higher good.

PART FIVE
Emergence of the Authentic Self

Chapter 26
Learning Curve

It could be that I'm slightly dense. Or, it could be that the Universe has felt compelled to show me a life bullet-pointed by extreme situations. Either way, my personal learning curve has definitely changed over the years. What began as a fairly unremarkable childhood has transformed into a life that now surprises me.

I always hated that despicable report we were forced to write in elementary school, "What I did on my Summer Vacation." I dreaded it because I didn't do anything remarkable. I spent my summers in an air-conditioned house watching *Mr. Ed*, *The Dick Van Dyck Show*, and *The Jetsons*. I drank Hawaiian Punch and ate corn dogs and Sloppy Joes. As an only child in a rural country setting, I played alone in my room pretending to be on television. I got to be both the host and guest on my own imaginary talk show as I alternated between interviewing and being interviewed. The former activity was a "Preview of Coming Attractions," minus the carb-loading. Little did I know one day I'd be doing this activity as a professional career.

As for my summer vacations, I never did anything spectacular. I just hung out. There are only two seasons in Minnesota. A freezing cold winter that lasts for nine months and a brief humid, hot summer. I'd hear reports from other kids (not too many mind you, as it was Minnesota) that had incredible adventures. They'd gone on trips to foreign countries like Canada or had been bitten by a snake. Eating junk food and watching TV didn't look like much by comparison. I wanted a big life but I wasn't old enough to drive a car.

Then, something happened. Adolescence allowed for new associations and experiences that challenged my thinking. Life began moving quickly. I made new friends from a wide array of artistic disciplines. I was active in theatre and began singing jazz with a local pianist. I was exposed to social movements and varied ideologies of thought that were both novel and thrilling. Life was no longer tame, predictable or ordinary. The onslaught of new information created a disposition of receptivity.

By adulthood, I'd developed a sense of comfort with what appeared as "different." Each situation would be measured by its outcome and evaluated according to its merit. I found that sharp contrast had the ability to catalyze new concepts and attitudes. Life seemed clearer when highlighted by extremes. The extremes were so obvious that even a moron couldn't miss the information garnered. There was an added benefit to life in extremes; it exempted formula answers. Each new segment of my life began to jump radically either in terms of interest and/or career. Now, I hunted the wild card and learned how to extract the essence from it.

Chapter 27
Our Beliefs

If you want to know what you think, look at your life. If you want to know what you believe, look at your life. You are currently living the out-picturing of your beliefs. Any limitations you may encounter are not only challenges for your greater development but also opportunities for your growth.

It is our beliefs that need to be expanded in order to actualize the life we see inside our minds and hearts. Choosing to expand our beliefs is the key to changing our world. It is in breaking through the limitations of our socio-environmental conditioning that we increase our abundance of health, prosperity, love and happiness. Limitation and fear are the opposite of abundance and faith. In keeping with the metaphysical mechanics of life, where we put our attention becomes the reality we experience. There are dark days and difficult passages. There are problems and challenges. But it's in the approach of our belief system and the subsequent thinking that we can turn the darkest situation into one that renders gold.

Wherever we are now in our beliefs, the message we need to understand is that we are able to expand that vision. Today's top of the ceiling is tomorrow's foundation. Change doesn't take years. It can happen in a matter of seconds. That is evolution. We are intrinsically programmed to be more, and create more. We are designed for continual growth. It is only when we stunt these natural urges to advance that we are forced to experience pain.

If we don't actively seek out new challenges, new challenges will seek us out. If we don't actively look within ourselves, events/ situations will *force* us to delve within. Our beliefs are the only things that can aid us or harm us. Our beliefs are what we assign them to be. If we choose to absorb the external, pre-fab information as our only compass, then that compass will lead us to what we already know. By expanding what we believe to be possible, we expand the truth of that becoming our reality. By allowing another set of options by which to assess our information, we gain another set of outcomes. We are only limited by our own thinking. And that can always evolve.

Chapter 28
Transformation

The transformation of the self may sound like an outside job, but it's actually an inner liberation of who we are *already*. Transformation is the process of uncovering the gem within and allowing it to shine. Each gem is unique; no cut, shape, size, or color is exactly alike. That's the beauty of the real self. There is only one. It's our gift to the world and to our selves.

It takes awareness to uncover the true self, and a willingness to allow for transformation. At times it can appear that the person we want to become is so very far from our reach. Inherent within each of us lies the real self, waiting to be released from the bondage of scripts, limitation and lack of belief. The true self is unlimited; it is all potential realized and all dreams accomplished. It's the individual expression of our unique creation and personal vision. We already have the gift within.

The physical world is in opposition to our truth. We have been taught to seek our inner selves by looking outward. We've been conditioned to emulate certain prototypes of success and programmed to adopt a pre-formed value system in order to become productive individuals. Prescribed costumes of compliance abound, with variations tailored to each segment of society.

Getting to the real self is simply peeling back the false layers that encage us. It's getting in tune with our authentic feelings and discovering our passion. By examining our inner tapes, social scripts and programming, an analysis can be made. We can become aware of those things that work for us, and those that feel false. The false identities and beliefs that have been heaped on us by our social scripts and inner tapes need to be identified, demystified, and released. No guilt, no shame; just the recognition of our true core and our heart's desire that lies within. This is the point of transformation. We begin to listen to our gut, our heart, and our own voice. Most of the old and unwanted must die. There will be a death cycle followed by the void. The void is the place of nothingness that connects death to new life. It's the cold winter that appears lifeless yet the seeds of all nature's wonders are gaining strength before their springtime emergence.

By trusting the magnificence of nature's design we can see the beauty in our own transformational cycles. The cycles, if we allow them to take us, push us forward in our personal evolution. We need to be willing to be the ugly duckling in order to become the swan.

Chapter 29
It's all About You

I had chosen the most remote part of New Jersey in which to build a weekend home. It wasn't meant to replicate a New York City lifestyle with a vibrantly diverse community or cultural enhancement. It was meant to provide tranquility and escape. A year later it became my full time residence. Part of me loved the comforts of a real home resplendent with nature as opposed to the confinement of an urban apartment. Though the physical environment was expansive and nurturing, my spirit slowly shriveled. I needed connection to people with bigger visions to reignite my dreams and passion. Yet in that solitude and lack of stimulation, I found a deeper healing. I had time to think. Through journaling and meditation, my inward awareness had a profoundly positive effect. The known and the unknown came bubbling to the surface. The appropriate time had presented itself and in some instinctive way, I had chosen the correct location for this to happen. Once all the broken toys were lying at my feet and every method I had tried failed to mend them, I sought out the big guns.

I discovered a couple that taught metaphysics out of their home in a neighboring community. Like myself, they had lived and worked in Manhattan for years. Unlike my rural neighbors, they weren't afraid to drive east on Route 80 toward Manhattan. Their classes provided a powerfully stabilizing force. They spoke my language and understood my thinking. Individually, they were exciting, dynamic, and successful. As teaching partners, they were doubly effective. Both had taken the established curriculum that enabled them to work as licensed spiritual practitioners.

Each week the class began with a sharing session in which the students could discuss their challenges and revelations. Carolyn would lovingly apply the spiritual balm of her practice as Irv sat listening attentively. He was there to let his wife shine. When she'd fully expressed herself, Irv would add his take on the situation. As the creative director of a premiere international advertising agency his style of communication was straightforward, concise and grounded in the real world. He had a gift for the right words. This powerful yet supremely humble man had a knack for putting a killer tagline on his wife's analysis. Repeatedly, he would say to me, "It's all about you." His statement put a thorn in my side. It was like the feeling one experiences when they are pricked by the knowledge that something important had been said; something one doesn't understand but knows they should.

Several years later I came to understand the power of this concept. It's all about us. What we learn, what we discover, and all the stories we create in that process… it's all about us. The partners we choose, what they do or don't do—in the end, it's all about us. People and situations will continually provide the rub that chafes us; the way irritants chafe the oyster to create a pearl. The things that bother us are here to assist us. The people and situations that trigger us provide the divine possibility to deactivate our hot buttons. By continually clearing away our reactivity we take control of the self-perpetuating story we have created. This is our opportunity to deal with the self and evolve. No longer victims of an outer world that tosses our emotions about like leaves in a storm, we face our issues head on. There is no getting around them because they will continue to haunt us in the future. If we try to repress them by pushing them into our past, they will erupt like an avalanche without warning. Left unattended they amass to form a cloud that distorts our vision of the world and its inhabitants.

What we are willing to discover and ultimately clear in our reactions is for *us*. It's for our growth and provides the ability to have a more objective understanding of life. By taking responsibility for inner issues triggered by outer events we unlock the gem that lies inside: the real person. The real person inside is powerful in understanding and compassion. We begin to see the actions of others with an impersonal eye. We are no longer triggered into attacking or condemning. When people act out unconsciously, we realize they're playing out the only responses they know. Acting out is based on control for gaining power. We recognize the underlying fear and powerlessness in this action, and separate the illusion from the reality.

Real power doesn't come by manipulating others. Real power doesn't use control. Real power is the knowledge of oneself and acting from the strength of that awareness. Real power is the humility to ask more of oneself and seek a better way to express (or not express) a reaction. It's the willingness to readjust and come out on a higher level. When an internal clearing has been done, the thorn is removed. Then it's not only all about us, but also for us.

Chapter 30
My Mother's Gift

I had a mother who never understood me until the end of her life. I'd wished our connection could have come sooner but it had its own timeframe. The delay was not for my lack of effort but because it was (how does one say this politely) a "challenging" relationship.

As a teenager, I wasn't the daughter she envisioned rearing. I was, at times, a social embarrassment for refusing to tow the line of WASP protocol. I blatantly ignored the script I'd been handed. I rejected the dance lessons and coming out party, and took a major detour from the prescribed path for which I was groomed. I ran away from the world of The Junior League, finger sandwiches, and "marrying well." I thought differently. I lived a different life. At that point in time my individualism was viewed as a rebellion.

I imagine my mother's corresponding level of concern. These were the traditional rites of passage to guarantee my place in the world; and that in my lack of insight I may never reap the benefits of acceptance gained through conformity.

There is a point where rebellion from what we don't want becomes clarification of what we do want. Resistant energy converts to forward movement in the discovery of a new form of expression. The marvelously crafted architecture here to advance our journey provides things to "push against." They provide the backdrop and impetus for moving towards the person we were meant to become. It was only in this remarkable set up that I discovered my real direction in life and my need to live by my own code.

I couldn't fathom a greater purpose for our mutual irritation with each other, at the time. I was too busy fighting for my beliefs to see the benefit of my mother's participation within the grand architecture of our dynamic. Without this chafe, there would be no distinction or passion to fuel my journey of self-discovery. Another gift of this dynamic was the need for clear self-expression. It forced me to think independently, to debate, and to substantiate my position. My adolescence was spent trying to find a language that would clarify my intentions to the mother who loved me, but was confused by my behavior. I eventually found a form of expression by which to communicate; to a woman who only knew the language she'd learned as she tenaciously held to the "scripts" she'd been given.

To repress the authentic self and don an appropriate costume may allow readmission to the group from which we came. But to live a life that is not authentic in a structure that confines one's spirit—is no life at all. The price for living one's "truth," may necessitate separation. It is only the separation from what feels false, that crystallizes entry to living a life, which feels correct. For those who must live their truth, because to do otherwise would be the death of their spirit, this is a different type of "rite of passage." It may involve dancing and parties, or be a withdrawal from all activities. It may be silent and internal, or make front-page news. It may be a temporary exit from the world until we've established our own solid identity. From that position, we can enjoy reconnection with any group we value.

Thinking differently has far fewer dramatic consequences today than it did in former times. We have evolved as a society. Far more latitude is given to those who make choices outside their social blueprints. With a growing segment of our population in expansion, we are entering an exciting time period. On the cusp of a great tipping point, the world is corresponding to the individual actions and augmented choices each of us is making. There is greater inclusion. That is the hallmark of true evolution.

Chapter 31
The Shift

In every foundational shift toward expansion there is a loss of some existent beauty in the old form. To advance, there is a price. But the need to move forward and break beyond the constraints of established ways is the nature of life. Adaptation and advancement are the keys to new life. There is always a struggle and always a price. There is a price for getting in and a price for leaving. The price for leaving the remnants of a group or thought system that is no longer representative of our truth, could result in losing the support of our family members and friends. We may need to part from established careers, marriages, and social systems that no longer endorse the vision of who we are to become. It's the powerful need of the inner spirit to grow that demands this departure.

There are new languages and systems not yet born that will eventually serve to contain these choices. These words, markers, and guideposts will illuminate the way for the new course to be taken. There will be a gathering of the dust as it settles. It will have a form. It will be given a name. It will create a context in which there will be understanding and validation. Time will create a unification that provides an image and context that is cohesive, formed, and solidified. There will be a moment of calm before the next storm. The winds will gather speed, the dust will blow and the structure that held the now identifiable forms will be challenged once again. These models will eventually erode and collapse only to be born again. This is the pattern of life. It's the death of the old and birth of the new.

We currently live in a shifting structure. As the old structure is being challenged, we divide into two definitive camps. There are those who struggle to reinforce the existing models and those who want to destroy all remnants of its form. There is beauty in the old as it contains much that is good and valuable. We don't need to scrap all of it for the attainment of a better system. But when new structures are to be built, it's often the choice to clear the ground completely. This is where I advise caution.

This is where we can look for another approach to avoid the polarization of black and white thinking. If we fuse new thinking into the shift while retaining the structure, we have options. By identifying the elements from the old model that resonate for us, we can integrate them into the new model. It's like building a new home. There are older pieces of furniture we love and the knick-knacks that have sentimental value. Do we really need to discard everything that isn't current? Perhaps these items can be blended into the new environment. If we're willing to break rules, why not start with breaking the rule that states everything has to be either old, or new?

Chapter 32
It Wasn't the Party Dress that Chafed Me

"When does your mom come in to beat us?" I asked. Val laughed and told me I was crazy. I put my head back on the pillow but didn't sleep. I waited as I had every night, wondering. Is tonight the night? How long will it last? How bad will it be?

I was in 7th grade when I stayed over night at Val Blazer's house. She was happy. Dinner was fun. Dishes weren't broken. Her mom didn't scream. Her family was laughing and smiling. My stomach didn't hurt. I was certain they were hiding something. Perhaps they were putting on a show for my benefit. I waited for "the other shoe" to drop. It didn't. What was this new experience?

Children of physical violence have no reference for an alternative reality. We know what we know. Certainly, that must be the Truth. With "no-talk" rules established to protect my father from the heart attack I gave him when I was in 2nd grade, I assumed everyone lived this way. My mother didn't gain her sobriety until I was sixteen. It took me several decades to release the imprint of actions that'd been seared into my heart.

Every human being who walks this physical life does so with his/her own set of challenges. No one escapes pain. At some point we will all face our own form of crisis. Struggling to master health or money issues, death or divorce, we all get something that necessitates our transformation and transcendence. We may experience severe social discrimination or life-threatening political upheaval. Each of us must develop our own manner of healing and perfecting our skill at overcoming what has occurred.

To ask for a life of gray is a pointless goal. Life has all colors and each have their values. To diminish the ability to feel in order to eliminate pain is a route I chose not to take. To transform what I experienced and make all that I could of it, was the way I found that worked for me. Our choices are as unique and varied as we are, as individuals.

There are no right answers. There are only those answers that work for us. The course of action one chooses at a given point in time may need re-calibration at a later date. Life is evolving, and we are all finding our own way in a manner that agrees with our inner directives. My choices may be different or similar to other's choices and should be of no consequence to anyone but me.

In my forties I felt the overriding need to see my mother with new eyes; to be able to see the human beyond my remembrance of the person, and to see if in doing that I might find someone else beyond what I had known. This was not done to alleviate her pain, but mine. Not born of denial or compliance, but born of an active choice in the hopes of personal liberation. Not to agree with what happened but to use what I was given and find a form by which to heal myself. I did that. Gradually, a new woman emerged. In unlocking my remembrance of her, she was freed to become the mother she had always wanted to be for me.

This is the woman who died in my arms. The woman, who couldn't cry, yet wept in the transit to death as she fixed her gaze on me. Without the ability to speak, I heard the flood of dialogue she held within. Her burden was far greater than mine. I didn't carry the memory of those actions. She couldn't release them. I led her as far as I could to wherever she was going; knowing I'd gained a mother and myself in the process. Understanding that love is unending, and that our experience of it comes in many forms and variations.

I'll never know the demons within another person, nor will I ever know the extremity of the events they've endured that created their personality. I will only know my experience of them. In each moment and each situation, I will make the decision as to how I proceed, or not. That is the freedom I have found in trusting myself. It is from that knowing that our greatest gifts may be realized.

PART SIX
Living the Greater Design

Chapter 33
The Cards We Hold

I have a wide array of friends and associates. They have vastly different philosophical positions; this diversity delights me in its ability to keep me alert and aware. Some friends are deeply spiritual. Others are decidedly atheist, humanist or agnostic. Some believe we choose our family of origin, and agree to all the challenges we encounter as a method of advancing our soul's transit through pre-life planning. Other colleagues believe there is nothing before our life begins and nothing that follows. Compelling arguments for both positions abound.

As for myself, I choose to stay open to all information. Regardless of the occurrences before or after life, my attention has been focused on living this current experience in the best manner possible. The tools I've found to be of greatest benefit have been disclosed in this book, as they work consistently and effectively. They do so regardless of one's philosophical viewpoint.

No matter what the nature of your personal belief, the fact remains: we are living *this* life. Whether we chose our challenges or they were thrust upon us, we must play the cards we've been dealt. Those cards are the ones we drew at birth. They contain our family of origin, talents, and difficulties. They color our position in the world and define the things that we must transcend. We may like or hate the hand that we drew. It doesn't matter. We can work with what we've been given when we understand that all the cards have value. We have some cards that are obviously strong. And we have in our possession those, which baffle us. As in, "Now really, what the hell am I supposed to do with this card?"

We come into this life with certain strengths and gifts. We also have obvious challenges. That's the beauty of the mixture of the cards in our hand. The only question we need to ask is, "How can I make the most of the hand I'm holding? Given the cards I've been dealt, how can I use these factors to bring my life to its greatest expression and contribution?"

Oddly, and quite stunningly, we discover the cards we hated are the ones that serve us best. The challenges carve our soul's purpose and the talents we possess bring that purpose forward. It's a magnificent design, all of which is crafted for our ultimate advancement. Whatever we thought was withheld, is what we will activate in a manner that can never be eradicated. Whatever has been stolen from us is ours to give back to ourselves and to share with the world. Whatever we assumed was our greatest defect, we can mold into its perfect opposite reflection. We soon discover that no matter what cards we drew we are in complete possession of the finest version of any hand possible. We see the purpose in the cards we drew and activate their power as we discover our power, through them.

Chapter 34
Disconnecting to Reconnect

The act of disconnecting from the limited self to the expansive self is done in stages. First, we disconnect from black and white thinking. In doing so, the analysis of what is perceived to be reality, changes. When thought systems are opened to greater choices than win/lose, up/down, the summation of all events shift to a higher realm.

Systems with limited options and outcomes necessitate winners and losers. The anxiety of that roller coaster ride, who's up and who's down, becomes our own private death. There's a momentary sense of confidence when we're on top and winning our agenda. Then, we crash in a downward spiral with the turn of the tide. Our gain is brief, as the outcome is constantly shifting. The mercurial effects of an ego in peril consume tremendous amounts of human energy. A joyous life is not possible when one is mentally invested in the ego. A joyous life is possible when one is free from thought systems that demand these ego-based responses.

In disconnecting from the inner tapes and default modes that color our reaction to events/situations, we expand the possibility of seeing life's events with fresh eyes. Very little of what we experience is personalized. Our objectivity increases. Our response to events and situations shifts. We discover the life we already have is richer than we imagined.

As we disconnect from the social scripts that defined who we were in the world, we begin to grow into our true selves. It is in this disconnection that we are able to fully reconnect with life. We discover a new sense of confidence in living our truth. We honor our skills and their manner of expression. We know our value, and the value of our life choices.

Disconnecting from these pre-programmed constructs frees us from reactivity. No longer tossed about by outer stimuli and no longer needing to control our outer world, we may now focus on our own advancement. With lessened reactivity to others, deeper levels of human connection are forged. We can begin to appreciate the remarkable beauty in the people we know, as well as those we meet.

As personal awareness increases, we continue to untangle the knots that bound our energetic life force. There is another way of seeing our world, who we are, and who we can become. There is a greater understanding of the events/situations that unfold around us as the magnificence of a greater design reveals itself. There is always the possibility of magic. That magic only occurs in the fertile soil of an open mind and an open heart.

Here to assist our highest expression and manifestation, the divine life-energy continues to provide more events/situations for our advancement. Each moment is limited only by our perception. The ability to attain higher levels of understanding and perceive higher outcome is a viable reality, available to everyone, at all times. As we learn more information, more is available to us. As we see beyond the *appearance* of what is, greater dimensions are revealed.

This is only the beginning. Greater discoveries will be made and greater dimensions will be reached. As our perspective contin-ues to broaden, our knowledge of reality will alter in accordance. There is no limit to who we can become and what we can achieve once we have freed ourselves to reconnect with the power of our own life force.

Chapter 35
And It's Not About You

Irv was correct. It's all about us. We choose the filter through which we see our life and through which we create our reality. We create the stories that perpetuate our beliefs. The art of self-awareness eliminates reactivity to outer stimuli. It allows us to finally see, what we are actually seeing. Without distortion, we can think independently and respond from a secure self.

While we're busy creating our own reality, so are others. And, as you may have noticed… not everyone is actively working on themselves. Until the inner work has been done the outer world will hold those unaware, captive. Life is lived in auto-response to the fluctuations of each new event. Just tune into any reality television show to see how this works.

There are times it's not always about us. People exist in varied states of self-awareness. Reactions are learned and people do what they do, because that's all they know. Limited tools create limited choices. Other people's issues, drama and acting out, aren't always about us. Nor are they always in response to our direct causation. Only in the act of discernment would we be able to decipher our participation, or lack of thereof, in creating the events/situations we witness. The only way to know if anything in our energy created the observed dynamic is to check into our reactions. If the situation catalyzed a "charge" within us, we clearly assisted in that scenario. Then, there is indeed something for us to learn and re-calibrate.

When triggered by a person or situation the automatic response is to react. We've been programmed (like everyone else) to this default reaction. But here is where we can choose to change our pre-conditioning. We can take a breath, and *think*. We don't need to bite the bait until we've checked in with ourselves. We can choose to pause and think, rather than automatically respond.

When we know our truth, we become an impartial witness who simply watches the actions of others. That witness separates what is *their* truth, from what is *our* truth. The level of reactivity to other's attitudes is minimized as we distinguish that which does not belong to us. Personalization of the event is bypassed. There is the ability to self-correct rather than having to correct those around us. We will always have issues that arise. But now, there is awareness in that observation. We can clearly see the difference between what is "their stuff" and what is "our stuff." We take responsibility for adjusting ourselves rather than chastising them.

We can indeed live the reality we desire. We have the ability to be pro-active rather than auto-responsive. We hold the master key to unlock our lesser learning and actualize our own greater design. Within each of us is the one who knows and sees what is possible, in the presence of that which appears to the contrary.

Chapter 36
Social Evolution of Identity

What we know about our social identity is constantly expanding. As individuals continue to evolve in their own consciousness, that awareness catalyzes the greater expansion of our entire social paradigm. As each human seeks the fullness of his or her life's expression, tremendous advancements are being realized; that input is incorporated into the larger social template.

Mid-twentieth century thinking assumed "all is well." Families portrayed in the media were happily functional, as housewives gleefully vacuumed their homes in dresses. Social convention was polite and predictable. Personal concerns were confined to external factors such as sickness, death or financial strife. Human discontent could be alleviated by "buying happiness" in the form of a new washing machine, or automobile.

By the 1960s and 1970s, the underpinnings began to weaken. A country that was at war and divided in its ideology pushed the political/cultural context to include a more realistic image of life. The emergence of another story was weaving its way into the fabric of the larger social narrative. The need for individual rights, inclusion, and validation went beyond any single group of race, gender or sexual orientation; as participating fully in life became a necessity for all.

The twentieth century marked the shift from denial to uncomfortable self-awareness. As the gaze turned inward, people discovered they had issues independent of external events. From this new template the death of innocent denial prompted many to look within, as a form of healing. Pop-psychology, spirituality and treatment facilities went mainstream to address the myriad of newfound issues. Divided opinions from leaders in each field made the transit confusing. Spiritual teachers advised forgiveness and prayers for one's abusers while therapists advised, "no-contact." Some schools of thought embraced self-identification through these wounds while others advised complete disassociation.

This new portrait of social identity added broad strokes of shocking color as the dimensional canvas widened. It was closer to an accurate image, but still incomplete. People could now identify their issues but could they move beyond their pain? The lure to capitalize on this growing market segment led some healing factions to enter "victim commerce." While many programs and teachers were credible and sincere, the door had now flung wide open to include the bizarre and fraudulent, as the demand to recover inner peace became enticingly lucrative turf.

The twentieth century concluded with the awareness that people have complex inner lives and autonomous realities. The best advice that could be offered at that time was an understanding that traumatic events did indeed occur. Now there was a voice for all that were formerly mute. Yet, recognition of these inner-wounds left many individuals without definitive tools by which to transform all that was "bad" into that which could become "good." Therapeutic communities and spiritual philosophies did their best to heal these wounds but were hard-pressed to remove the lingering pain. The tools needed for true release and transformation were not available to the greater informational databank, though many tried in earnest to assist in whatever means they knew, at the time.

Today, the portrait of our social identity holds both light and dark colors, and many tones of gray intermixed. It is more complete, as we clearly see the things we need to fix and the things that are intact. As individuals advance, their greater community also advances in its inclusivity of awareness and understanding. It's the pathway for the evolution of our social identity. Enormous amounts of new information appear, altering the collective portrait in response to the human request for more colors and richer tones. Those inclusions make their way into the mainstream, thus allowing the mainstream to expand.

The age of denial moved through uncomfortable awareness toward an age of psychological fusion. Each time period holds its unique reality. Once that reality has been incorporated into the greater social fabric, it must change again. We have deepened immensely as a culture in discovering a truer version of what is real. People are gaining a wider worldview through which to see life and a deeper knowledge of their own inner workings. Individuals wanting authenticity and freedom are resistant to accept less than a life that resonates with their inner code.

We are only as advanced as the tools we hold. When the time comes that current issues eclipse our given tool set, we will create new tools. Without the ability to see beyond what *appears to be*, all the wounds that individuals carry can only be blanketed, but not alchemized. The healing tools are held within the awareness of how the greater design utilizes all events/situations to move us forward. The wounds sustained remain intact if not understood beyond limited thinking. Since all events/situations are either deemed good or bad, by that kind of analysis, the wounds must live on forever. To liberate the image of the wounds, a master tool needs to be available by which to remove the injury. That tool is the application of reviewing the impact of causation, and reframing the event in a broader context. That master tool is the gift of a greater design.

Chapter 37
Snow on the Car Roof

Getting to our core truth and its realization is a process. Some call it the peeling of the onion, as we systematically remove the false layers that cover the true self. I see it as driving behind a car that has snow on its roof.

With the forward movement of the car, clumps of snow start to fly off the roof. It begins as a light powdery dust that blows easily off the car with minimal acceleration. This is the most recent snow, still soft and fresh as it hasn't had time to harden. Then, the bigger clumps begin to release. In very little time, there is a dramatic difference. The car appears free of snow. Yet, hidden from obvious sight is the underlying ice that formed in the earliest parts of the snowfall. Like the frozen layers closest to the inner core of our true selves, it is the last to leave. Compressed by the weight of all that was on top, it is the bedrock that remains. It too will dissipate. The sun will warm the ice and melt away all remnants of its existence.

In order to chip away at the layers that cover our authentic self, the process required is one of "uncovering" that which hides the core. The core is always perfect. It is not a perfection for which one must strive or toil. It is the inborn magnificence that is the higher self. Compacted by years of false information, poison pabulum fed to us by a confused thought system and social scripts, the true self remains exquisite in its totality. We were born whole. We were born connected to the spirit within and spirit all around. It is the misunderstanding that has been heaped upon us that sends the message of separation of self, from higher self. The return to wholeness is not an arduous process but a continual reawakening to our birthright.

If there is only one message you get from this book, let it be the understanding that you are perfect as you are. You have always been perfect, and there are no mistakes to be made. The only thing that separates us from ourselves is the erroneous belief that we are somehow flawed or off-course. We are wise beyond our comprehension and have always been connected to our worthiness and contribution. We have been the unfortunate recipients of lesser information that has not kept pace with who we know ourselves to be. But now, all of that is changing as the world is moving closer to the valid truth of what we hold within our hearts to be the greater reality.

This life is neither a test, nor a question of our worth. We are not here to prove our capabilities or conform to scripts that are not true for us. We are worthy and valid in all we do, before outer recognition appears. We are only in a process, of living. It is in that process that we discover our contribution to the greater expansion of our world, adding in our version of life, as we live it.

Chapter 38
Getting Better, Looking Worse

There is an incongruity in the process of becoming whole. When we are able to uncover our inner tapes we must face the uncomfortable discovery of their content. We see our erroneous constructs. We can identify them. At this exact point, while enormous clarity has been gained, there is the attending feeling of greater troubles. We are getting better, but looking worse.

The sudden image of that which silently ruled our unconscious has just come forward to our attention. Now, we think we really have "problems." It's only an illusion. This is one of the many peculiarities of cognition. Realization is awareness. The act of awareness focuses the mind on that which was formerly hidden. Instead of viewing this information as a new batch of issues, the more accurate interpretation is that the hidden thoughts are being released. At this point of conscious awareness we are actually healthier than before.

When my friend Maurizio had finally cleared his life of alcohol, he thought his work was done. A year into sobriety he discovered a greater dependency, the need for social acceptance. The lure of status, fame, and prominence ruled his unconscious far more than evening cocktails had. As feelings of low self-worth came flooding to the surface he berated himself for being more screwed up than before, when he was actively drinking. Without understanding how to dismantle the underlying tapes his new lifestyle could never be maintained. By becoming conscious of his limiting thoughts, he could alter them. He relaxed and trusted the masterful ability of the body and mind to work in tandem. He began to base his self-worth on how he felt about himself, rather than external factors.

Maurizio's self-confidence grew tremendously as a result of this inner awareness.

One's "getting better" may initially appear like one is "looking worse." However, all the things floating to the surface are things we can see and therefore adjust. Their influence, when cloaked, may seem hidden from the light, but are never hidden from causation. Dismantling our inner tapes is a temporary discomfort in the process of gaining the true self. Getting better seems like a departure from where we want to be, and where we are headed. It's only temporary. Looking worse is the recognition that we have areas that must be adjusted. That's the good news. These are matters that are in our control. Awareness allows us to make our adjustments to inner tapes and social scripts. Without that awareness we would be in a perpetual state of default. As the light shines clearly on that which must be re-calibrated, we recognize our ability to alter our default reaction and have it serve us, rather than live in servitude to its directives.

Chapter 39
Uncovering the True Self

The process of uncovering the true self is less work than we imagine it to be. A single directly applied thought can change dozens of outer actions. When we think of change, in any form, the automatic assumption is that "change" is the end-result of a long, laborious process. This assumption is born of old-world thinking. To look at the self as something to be sought after, (as its parallel construct in the world of outer reference), implies it is another, outer form of a "better Self" that must be acquired. The true self doesn't exist outside of us. We own it.

It isn't a "different self" we must struggle to attain, incorporate, and reformulate. Just by mentally accepting the idea that we all have a true and perfect core enables the false layers that cover the true self, to be removed.

The true self is authentically ours. We were born with it intact. The only process required for realizing it, is the mental understanding that we own it; it is pure, intact, and already whole. When we learn to distinguish this fact from the false truth heaped upon us, we allow our perfection to emanate. The flaws we imagine to exist are not those of our being, but those of our misunderstanding. They are not organic, but have been acquired through living in a world that *tells* us who we are, rather than *sees* who we are.

I've met "class junkies." They are the people continually enrolled in lectures and workshops to learn about themselves. I've done it, too. But no teacher, no system, no ideology "OUT THERE," can tell you who you are inside. There is no guru, master, coach, teacher or trainer who can access the real you, except you yourself. There is no doctrine, sect, seer, healer, or practitioner, who can do your inner work for you. All are adjuncts to your journey. Even this book...

The best any book, friend, therapist, doctrine or method can do is to urge you forward and provide loving support. If they tell you otherwise—run, don't walk. No one has your power, and no one can sell it to you. No one owns your thoughts, and no one can give your thoughts to you. If you imagine your truth is out there somewhere—people, systems and doctrines will be happy to take your money and confuse your inner knowing. It's better for them that you don't know who you are. Docile, un-empowered and sub-missive to the manipulations of other's agendas, you can go along numbly living the life you are told to live at the expense of your heart and soul.

There is nothing wrong with knowing the power you possess and living like you know it. When it is real and true, it is always pure and generous. There is nothing wrong with wanting to be all that your spirit came here to be. It is your obligation to life. There is no one that can be you and no one who can replicate you. We are not here to replicate others. The most perfect expression of you is what you already *are*.

Don't look to the outer world to validate your inner truth's form and function. You won't find it there. How could you? It has never been seen before you were created to show its magnifi-cence. Like a beautiful eternal flame, your true self is always burning brightly. Covered by the false shrouds of inner tapes, social scripts, and learned beliefs, the glow may now appear faint. In removing the layers of misbeliefs and misunderstandings, the whole Self is allowed its resplendent glory. It is the spirit that shines within you and lights the way for others. It is your guide when in darkness and the compass to your true north.

Made in the USA
San Bernardino, CA
12 September 2016